THE RECRUITING OFFICER

George Farquhar

The Royal Court Writers Series
published by Methuen
in association with the Royal Court Theatre

ROYAL COURT WRITERS SERIES

First published as a paperback original in 1988 by Methuen Drama
Michelin House, 81 Fulham Road, London SW3 6RB

British Library Cataloguing in Publication Data
Farquhar, George, *1678-1707*
    The recruiting officer.————(Royal
    Court writers series).
    I. Title   II. Series
    822'.4

    ISBN 0-413-19630-5

Printed in Great Britain by Expression Printers Ltd, London N7 9DP

The front cover shows the 1774 election in the Square at Shrewsbury.
The picture is reproduced by courtesy of Rowley's House Museum, Shrewsbury.

The Royal Court Theatre
and Diana Bliss present

THE RECRUITING OFFICER
BY GEORGE FARQUHAR

MR BALANCE ⎫ Two Justices .... Mark Lambert
MR SCRUPLE ⎭ .... Jude Akuwudike
MR WORTHY, a gentleman of Shropshire........................Nigel Cooke
CAPTAIN PLUME, a recruiting officer............................Julian Wadham
CAPTAIN BRAZEN, a recruiting officer.................................Ron Cook
KITE, Sergeant to Plume...Clive Russell
BULLOCK, a country clown...Ron Cook
COSTAR PEARMAIN, a recruit.............................Jude Akuwudike
THOMAS APPLETREE, a recruit......................Kathryn Hunter
PLUCK, a butcher...Mark Lambert
BRIDEWELL, a constable...Nigel Cooke
SERVANT, to Justice Balance............................ Jude Akuwudike

MELINDA, a lady of fortune..............................Kathryn Hunter
SILVIA, daughter to Balance, in love with Plume....Amanda Redman
LUCY, Melinda's maid..Suzanne Packer
ROSE, a country wench....................................... Mossie Smith

ALL OTHER PARTS PLAYED BY MEMBERS OF THE COMPANY

Directed by....................................... Max Stafford-Clark
Designed by .... Peter Hartwell
Lighting by .... Christopher Toulmin
Sound by...Andy Pink
Costume Supervisor ....Jennifer Cook
Fight Arranger .... Terry King
Assistant Director................................ Philip Howard
Company Manager....................................Neil O'Malley
Stage Manager ....Jude Wheway
Assistant Stage Manager ....Gary Crant
Poster..Sightlines
Production photos..................................John Haynes

The play takes place in Shrewsbury in the late summer of 1704
following the Battle of Blenheim in August of that year.
There will be one interval of 15 minutes

Thanks to the Women's Playhouse Trust who helped take
THE RECRUITING OFFICER and OUR COUNTRY'S GOOD to Australia.

Wardrobe care by PERSIL and BIO-TEX. Adhesive by COPYDEX and EVODE LTD. Ioniser
for the lighting control room by THE LONDON IONISER CENTRE (836 0211). Cordless drill
by MAKITA ELECTRIC (UK) LTD. Watches by THE TIMEX CORPORATION. Batteries by EVER
READY. Refrigerators by ELECTROLUX and PHILLIPS MAJOR APPLIANCES LTD. Microwaves
by TOSHIBA UK LTD. Kettles for rehearsals by MORPHY RICHARDS. Video for casting
purposes by HITACHI. Cold bottled beers at the bar supplied by YOUNG & CO. BREWERY,
WANDSWORTH. Coffee machines by CONA.

Funded by

LONDON
BOROUGHS
GRANTS
SCHEME

FINANCIALLY ASSISTED BY THE
ROYAL BOROUGH OF
KENSINGTON AND CHELSEA

Arts Council Funded

BIOGRAPHIES

JUDE AKUWUDIKE — For the Royal Court: *The Recruiting Officer* and *Our Country's Good*. Other theatre includes: *The Park* (Sheffield Crucible); *Moon on a Rainbow Shawl* (Almeida); *The Fatherland* (Riverside). Film: *A World Apart*.

RON COOK — For the Royal Court: *The Arbor, Cloud Nine, The Grass Widow, Greenland, The Recruiting Officer* and *Our Country's Good*. Other theatre includes: *Sons of Light, Television Times, The Winter's Tale, The Crucible, The Dillen* (RSC); *She Stoops to Conquer* (Lyric, Hammersmith); *Ecstasy* and *How I Got That Story* (Hampstead); *Cock-Ups* (Royal Exchange, Manchester); *Three Sisters* (Greenwich/Albery). TV includes: *The Merry Wives of Windsor, A Day to Remember, The Singing Detective, The Miser, Bergerac*. Films: *The Cook, The Thief, His Wife and Her Lover, Number One*.

NIGEL COOKE — For the Royal Court: *Serious Money*, (at Wyndhams). Other theatre includes: seasons at Bristol Old Vic, the Little Theatre, Bristol, Basingstoke, Bolton, Scarborough; *The Public* (Stratford East); *The Duchess of Malfi* (Roundhouse); for the RSC: *Twelfth Night, Julius Caesar, Volpone*. TV includes: *Galloping Galaxies* and *Death of a Son*. Film: *Try Me*.

PETER HARTWELL — For the Royal Court: *The Glad Hand, Wheelchair Willie, Not Quite Jerusalem, The Genius, A Colder Climate, The Arbor, The Edward Bond Season, Operation Bad Apple, The Grass Widow, The Recruiting Officer, Our Country's Good, Icecream*. At the Royal Court and Public Theater, New York: *Rat in the Skull, Top Girls, Aunt Dan and Lemon, Serious Money* (also on Broadway). At the Theatre Upstairs: *An Empty Desk, Marie and Bruce, Seduced*. For Joint Stock: *Epsom Downs, Cloud Nine, The Ragged Trousered Philanthropists, Borderline, Crimes of Vautrin*. Other theatre includes: *She Stoops to Conquer, The Beaux' Stratagem* (Lyric, Hammersmith); *Serjeant Musgrave's Dance* (National); *Delicatessen* (Half Moon Theatre). Also work for Hampstead Theatre Club, Foco Novo, Newcastle and Liverpool Playhouses and the Canadian Stage Company, Toronto.

KATHRYN HUNTER — Theatre includes: *Romeo and Juliet* and *The Merchant of Venice (Watermill); The Square* and *Yes, Peut-être* (Edinburgh Festival); *A Little Like Drowning* (Hampstead); *The Hypochondriac* (Lyric, Hammersmith)I *Electra* and *All's Well that Ends Well* (Leicester Haymarket); *Abel Barebone, Playing with Fire, Noah's Wife* (Traverse, Edinburgh); *Anything for a Quiet Life* and *The Visit* (Théâtre de Complicité/Almeida).

MARK LAMBERT — For the Royal Court: *Ourselves Alone, Built on Sand, The Recruiting Officer* and·*Our Country's Good*. Other theatre credits include: *Red, Black and Ignorant* and *Juno and the Paycock* (RSC); *Patrick Pearse Motel* (Abbey Theatre); *Observe the Sons of Ulster Marching Towards the Somme* (Abbey Theatre and Hampstead); *Comedians* (Young Vic); *Candy Kisses* (The Bush). TV includes: *Caught in a Free State, The Young Ones, An Affair in Mind, Time After Time*. Films: *Champions* and *Prayer for the Dying*.

SUZANNE PACKER — For the Royal Court: *A Hero's Welcome*. Other theatre includes: *Topsey Turvey, Younger Brother's Son, Meg and Mog* (Unicorn); *Carmen Jones* and *Lady Be Good* (Crucible, Sheffield); *Power of Darkness, Playboy of the West Indies, Dreams with Teeth, To Kill a Mockingbird* (Contact, Manchester); *Little Shop of Horrors* (Leeds Playhouse); *Porgy and Bess* (Glyndebourne); *Fat Pig* (Leicester Haymarket); *To Kill a Mockingbird* (Greenwich); *Holly and the Magical Oak* (Brighton); *A Blow to Bute Street* (Cardiff). TV includes: *Bowen*.

AMANDA REDMAN — Theatre includes: *The Seagull, As You Like It, Destiny, A Month in the Country, Love for Love* (Bristol Old Vic); *The Rocky Horror Show, Windy City (West End); Crimes of the Heart* (Bush); *The Duenna* and *Swan Esther* (Young Vic); *Private Lives* (Oxford); *State of Affairs* (Lyric, Hammersmith); *Love for Love* (National); *The Last Waltz* (Greenwich). TV includes: *La Ronde, Pericles, Oxbridge Blues, To Have and to Hold, The Rivals, Bergerac, The Importance of Being Earnest, Streets Apart, The Lorelei*. Films include: *Richard's Things, Give My Regards to Broad Street, For Queen and Country*.

CLIVE RUSSELL — For the Royal Court: *Keeping Body and Sould Together.* Other theatre includes: Nine years in TIE/Community Theatre; *Kiss and Kill, Scum, Teendreams* (Monstrous Regiment); *Accidental Death of an Anarchist* (Wyndhams); *Hamlet, Waiting for Godot, A Streetcar Named Desire, Enemy of the People* (Lancaster); *Dracula, Scrap, The Erpingham Camp, Macbeth, Alfie* (Liverpool); *No Paseran, Macbeth, A View from the Bridge* (Young Vic); *King Lear* (Old Vic); for the RSC: *Philistines, The Dillen, Troilus and Cressida, Mephisto, Heresies, Principae Scriptorae, Fashion, New Inn, A Question of Geography, The Bite of the Night.* TV includes: *Boys from the Blackstuff, Anarchist, Tumbledown* and *The Gift.*

MOSSIE SMITH — For the Royal Court: *Shirley, Road, The Recruiting Officer, Our Country's Good.* Other theatre includes: *The Crucible* (Young Vic). TV includes: *Triangles, Number 10, Reith, Rat in the Skull, Putting on the Ritz, Road* and *A Very Peculiar Practice.*

MAX STAFFORD-CLARK — Like George Farquhar, Max Stafford-Clark is a graduate of Trinity College, Dublin. He was Artistic Director of the Traverse Theatre, Edinburgh, from 1968-1970. In 1972 he founded the Joint Stock Theatre Group and in 1979 he became Artistic Director of the Royal Court.

CHRISTOPHER TOULMIN — Resident Lighting Designer at the Royal Court for 7 years. For the Royal Court: *Falkland Sound, Aunt Dan and Lemon, The Grace of Mary Traverse, Ourselves Alone, Road, A Lie of the Mind, The Recruiting Officer, Icecream.* Other theatre includes: *The Seagull* (Sherman, Cardiff); *Gaudete* (Almeida); *Cosi Fan Tutte* (Scottish Opera); *Mary Stuart* (Greenwich); *School for Scandal* (Bristol Old Vic); *Ghost Sonata* (Opera Factory); *Roots, The Father, Bed* (National Theatre); *Making History* (Field Day, National Theatre); several productions at Liverpool Playhouse.

JULIAN WADHAM — For the Royal Court: *Serious Money, Falkland Sound, Young Writers' Festival.* Other theatre includes: *Mountain Language, The Changeling* (National Theatre); *When We Are Married, Another Country* (West End); also seasons at Chichester, Ipswich, Leatherhead, Leeds. TV includes: *Blind Justice, Baal, Country, Bright Eyes, The Guest, Bergerac, The Gentle Touch.* Films: *Mountbatten* — the *Last Viceroy* and *Maurice.*

JULIAN WADHAM & RON COOK IN THE RECRUITING OFFICER

PHOTO: BRANCO GAICA

LETTERS TO GEORGE

By Max Stafford-Clark

In August, Nick Hern Books will publish Max Stafford-Clark's first book, *Letters to George*. It takes the form of a correspondence with the author of *The Recruiting Officer*. In this book, Max traces the process of research and rehearsal on both *The Recruiting Officer* and Timberlake Wertenbaker's *Our Country's Good*.

Monday 20th June, 1988

We went to Shrewsbury today. Caught the 7.40am from Euston. Jude missed the train. Bacon rolls. Did the actions on the train with Mossie and Lesley. We did Act V, Scene 1. I know this is essentially a comic scene but why is the Constable arresting them both? Could couples simply be done for fornication? Has the Constable really misunderstood the contents of his warrant? Either way Silvia/Wilful is in trouble having supposedly debauched Rose. We speculate on what went on the night before . . . probably Wilful has supplied enough liquor to get everybody confused and arranges some sort of impromptu marriage service to satisfy Bullock and quieten Rose. They're probably all a bit hungover. We finish the scene by Birmingham New Street. At Wolverhampton, our Class 86 Electric is taken off and replaced with an old Bush 47 for the final leg to Shrewsbury.

It seems a backwater, a weird market hill town built on a bend in the river. The bridge into the town is called English Bridge and the bridge out, the other side, to the West, is Welsh Bridge. It's still a border town. Funny accents. Some distinctly Welsh . . . some very Birmingham . . . and quite a lot of the English country bray, that I 'm sure you would remember. Mark's accent for Pluck suddenly appears absolutely accurate and extremely well-researched. Because it's hemmed in by the river, the town hasn't grown much. In fact, the Victorian station is built on a large bridge slung across the river . . . there's no room for it anywhere else. The town is dominated by the Castle, which has now been turned into a military museum. We went there first. Leslie and Mossie claimed to have found the site of Plume's secret rendez-vous with Molly. It was an old gardener's hut. We saw the uniforms which were very vivid and charismatic. The Shropshire Light Infantry had most of their campaign experience in India. Very Kipling. Very Brecht. We get a lecture on the grass in the Castle Yard from Mr. Pritchard, the

ON THE TRAIN TO SHREWSBURY

custodian. It seems uniforms hadn't necessarily been invented at the time you came to Shrewsbury . . . still, I think we're likely to stretch a point here. We asked eagerly for The Raven, the coaching inn where you stayed and wrote the first draft and where Kite sets up the drinks in the first scene. Mr. Pritchard looked shifty. "I'm afraid you've just missed it . . ." he said, "it was knocked down sixteen years ago to make a Woolworths." All Salopians speak of its passing with some degree of shame. Ironically, Woolworths itself is to be knocked down soon to make way for the Charles Darwin Hypermarket. It turns out you're not Shrewsbury's most famous son after all, George. In fact, I'm sorry to say that in all the town guides we picked up you're mentioned only once. The Market Square, where you set both recruiting scenes is recognisable enough and the fine riverside walks with their beeches and elms would be probably as you remember them and as they were when Melinda stalked Worthy and Brazen duelled with Plume.

I suppose most important is the feeling of a tight, smug little market town, very English, rather friendly, gone a bit Benetton and rather pleased with itself. It's attractive, but not so pretty that it's on the tourist circuit. We were taken round Rowley House, a fine old merchant's town mansion, by Vivien Bellamy, the curator of the Shrewsbury Museum Service. She and her husband showed us Clive of India's house too. He was the local M.P. for a while, although he never lived in Shrewsbury much. We rehearsed the recruiting scene in the Market Square. You can see the two church clocks Kite orders poor Costar and Thomas to stand guard over. St. Chads fell in a storm in 1788, but the

OFF MARKET SQUARE

tower is still standing and there was an exhibition of local paintings that I went to look at . . . largely rather colourful landscapes. In the little park, where the church used to stand, two girls were having an early lunch and eating their sandwiches.

There's two streets of very nice town houses hard by St. Chads. Apparently, Shrewsbury was big enough to have its own season, but so small that everybody must have known each other intimately. Some questions we've been asking about the play are answered immediately. How well could Silvia have known Worthy? Very well indeed. How big is the the scandal about Molly? Pretty mega. How easily could Melinda avoid Worthy? With difficulty. How much has

MELINDA'S NEW HOUSE?

Shrewsbury been concerned about the romance between Plume and Silvia? They haven't talked about anything else all summer. In fact, I'm surprised they're not talking *still*. The headline in the local newspaper was "Shrewsbury Men May Have Been Involved in Truck Crash"! We found Melinda's apartment, Worthy's rather substantial town house and the even bigger mansion Melinda has her eye on now she's inherited 1.2 million pounds.

But the biggest triumph was Justice Balance's town house. I'm sure you will remember it. Just outside the castle walls, within a stone's throw of The Raven, is Council House Close. This name has rather confusing associations for us, but you will remember that it referred to The Council of the Welsh Marches. In this little square are two exquisite Queen Anne townhouses with a brick facade built over the wattle-and-daub of a much earlier building. They were completed in 1707 so I like to think they were quite a talking point when you were in town. They give a very clear idea of perfect balance and scale (to borrow your harmonious phrase for a moment, George). Vivien had arranged for Dr. Ireland, the kindly owner, to show us around. A retired G.P., his house was a wonder. The rooms were sizeable but not imposing, with dark oak panelling extending up to the ceilings. The dining room had a cupboard concealed in the panelling for the potty that gents would use when the ladies had withdrawn. I immediately remembered a passage from Roy Porter: "back in the 1660's, Pepys had thought nothing of defecating into a fireplace (servants cleared up the mess) and had himself caught Lady Sandwich 'doing something on the pot' in the dining room." Upstairs, the master bedroom had a beautiful four-poster bed with an immaculate white lace coverlet. The sash window revealed a sweeping vista down to the Severn with Mrs Ireland at work in the walled vegetable garden. The dressing room to the master bedroom had a double cupboard with a discreet hole concealed within it. This permitted the servants to empty the potty while the master and mistress still slumbered.

DR DUDLEY IRELAND IN HIS QUEEN ANNE HOUSE
(c.1710) OVERLOOKING THE SEVERN

Dr. Ireland took us into the terraced garden . . . a weeping willow looked over delphiniums, stocks, lilies, canterbury bells and roses. This was the vision of England that Plume must have yearned for sweating through the dark night before Blenheim. All this and eager Silvia too. I'd give up my hopes of being frigging general alright.

We said goodbye to Dr. Ireland and split up with two hours to kill before our train back. I wandered through the town once more, past The Raven (Woolworths) and down Shoemakers' Row.

SHOEMAKERS ROW

Pride Hill has been turned into a pedestrian centre and I sat on the bench listening to the different accents. Outside Boots a lad was fingering his guitar rather hopefully. The medieval street names, Dogpole, Mardall, Shop Latch, Wyle Cot, Old Fish Street, looked down on the shifting swell of T-shirted shoppers pushing prams and sucking ice-creams. Down the hill, I saw Jim and Nick absorbing the local atmosphere and talking to two girls. They've recognised Jim from his TV series. They sent Jude off to the local Army recruitment centre as a punishment for being late. Already I began to recognise faces: the three punks we had seen in the pub at lunchtime, the two lads working on the hole in the road with their arses hanging out of the back of their jeans that Mossie had been so struck by. It's a small town and the glamorous eruption of the red-coated, beer-swilling heroes of Blenheim must have been sensational. There's no way in a place this size that Silvia could miss Plume or remain unaware of what he's up to. There must have been real alarm too that Kite and Plume would disrupt the even balance of the town too much. Act V, Scene 2, which we tackle tomorrow, begins with this debate in progress between Justice Balance and Justice Scale. Scale is alive to his paternalistic responsibilities: "I say 'tis not to be borne, Mr Balance. This poor girl's father is my tenant, and if I mistake not, her mother nursed a child for you; shall they debauch our daughters to our faces?"

A complicated network of obligations, relationships and alliances connected all sections of the community. I think that's why it's such a wonderful play, George . . . because it moves out of London and, within the framework and conventions of a comedy, captures how much your play owes to your time in Shrewsbury. Janes writes: "that *The Recruiting Officer* really owes more to Farquhar's experiences in the theatre than it does to his experiences in Shrewsbury . . . it grows out of materials, forms and throughts that Farquhar worked with all during his career."

I would say that the play's real success is the way it uses the one experience to depict the other.

An extract from *Letters to George* — the account of a rehearsal.
Copyright © 1989 by Max Stafford-Clark.
Published by Nick Hern Books, 87 Vauxhall Walk, London SE11.

THE FULL COMPANY ON CLARK ISLAND, SYDNEY, AUSTRALIA. JUNE 1989.

1755

There were strict laws concerning the 'Poor' at this time, and the case of Jane Morris gives an interesting example of how the law was carried out in the case of an illegitimate child. There is little doubt that her pregnancy came about as a result of the Stretton May Fair jollifications in May 1755. 'Following her Examination and a Complaint by the Churchwardens of Hope Bowdler that her child had been chargeable to the Parish since its birth and would continue to be so, the two Justices of the Peace in the name of His Majesty King George the Second commanded the Petty Constable of Hope Bowdler "to convey ye said Jane Morris from your sd Township of Hope Bowdler to ye House of Correction at Salop and deliver her to the Master thereof and you the sd Master of ye sd House of Correction are hereby required to receive the sd Jane Morris into your sd House and her safely keep to hard labour for one whole year".'

Fordritishope, The Story of a Shropshire Parish.

1707

Ann Pilkington to be privately whipt and imprisoned until she finds out the mother of a bastard child left at Drayton, or gives security for her appearance at next Sessions.

Quarter Sessions Orders, Shropshire.

1815

'Moreover the weapons they (the officers) and the sergeants carried, swords and halberds, though of little offensive value, were exactly what was needed to keep individual soldiers, or groups of them, from running away. In one of General Lejeune's paintings of a Napoleonic battle in which he fought, he has actually portrayed a French sergeant pushing against the back of one of the French ranks, using his halberd horizontally in both hands to hold the men in place. It is not improbable to think of British sergeants having done the same at Waterloo.'

John Keegan: THE FACE OF BATTLE

1706

... There was lately published a Comedy call'd 'The Recruiting Officer', to render this employment as odious as possible. Here one 'Captain' is represented as a notorious lyar, another as a Drunkard, one intreagues with Women, another is scandalously guilty of debauching them; and tho' the Serjeant was married to five Women before, yet the Captain persuades him to marry another, as a Cloak for such Roguery, to make up his Five Wives half a Dozen, and to cheat the Queen, by entering a child born on the day before into the Muster-Roll, and after all he stiles these Debaucheries 'an Air of Freedom, which People mistake for Lewdness, as they mistake Formality in others for Religion', and then proceeds in commending his own Practice, and exposing the other. In this Play the Officers are represented as quarrelsome, but Cowards. The Serjeant makes the Mob drunk to list them, gives two of them two Broad Pieces of Gold, for Pictures, and Finding the Money upon them, pretends that they are listed: At another Time he is ready to swear anything for the Good of the Service; and also persuades Men to list in the Disguise of a Conjurer, with most profane Language in Commendation of the Devil;

In this Play the Officers confess, that they greatly abuse the new listed Soldiers; Debauching of the Country Wenches is represented as a main Part of the Service; All the Private Centinels are guilty of stealing Horses, Sheep and Fowls, and the Captain desires, that he may have 'but one honest Man in the Company for Novelty's sake'. After this the Justices of the Peace are made the Jest of the Stage, for discharging their duty in listing of soldiers, and the Constable hath a Lash into the Bargain, that no one who serves his Country on this Occasion, may escape the Play-House Censure.
Arthur Bedford: THE EVIL AND DANGER OF STAGE PLAYS

1804

At Winchester, two of the party, Andrews and Peters, dressed as countrymen, and, acting as groundbait, went strutting about, playing all manner of pranks. Having attracted some rustics they offered to treat them and retired to a tent where, after a few pots of beer, they declared their intentions of enlisting, Peters spinning out 'a long rigmarole of how his eldest brother, who enlisted that day three years ago, was now a captain in India, as rich as a nabob'. The moment seemed propitious, so one man slipped out for the sergeant, who dropped in as if by accident. Andrews then offered a drink to the sergeant, and shook hands with him, and they all sat down to beer. Andrews formally volunteered to enlist; Peters rose in a jolly, off-hand way and offered to go with him. 'The shilling was put into each of our hands in the king's name and we gave three cheers.' Ten to one but two or three of the company followed suit. If not, the sergeant sat down and pulled out a fistful of money and a couple of watches. Then he presented the watches to the new 'king's men' on behalf of their company, while advancing part of their bounty, adding that there were eight vacancies for sergeants which such smart men could well hope to fill soon. The watches usually had an astonishing effect and secured three or more fish.
Roy Palmer (ed): THE RAMBLING SOLDIER

c.1760

'The chastity of women is of all importance, as all property depends on it ... between a man and his wife, a husband's infidelity is nothing ... Wise married women don't trouble themselves about infidelity in their husbands ... The man imposes no bastards upon his wife.'
Dr. Johnson

GEORGE FARQUHAR:
A BRIEF CHRONOLOGY

1677 Born in Londonderry, son of an impoverished Church of England clergyman.

1689 Presumably still in Londonderry during the Jacobite siege of the city from April to July (and claimed by his mother to have fought in the Battle of the Boyne in 1690).

1694 Entered Trinity College, Dublin, as a 'sizar' — receiving scant board and tuition in return for menial duties.

1696 Left Trinity College without his degree, and acted (indifferently, by all accounts) at the Smock Alley Theatre in Dublin, making his debut as Othello.

1697 Accidentally wounded another actor in a stage duel, and, apparently on the advice of his friend and fellow-actor Robert Wilks, left for London to try his fortune as a playwright.

1698 His first play, the comedy *Love and a Bottle* (published 1699), performed with moderate success at Drury Lane in December, and his anecdotal novella, *Adventures of Covent-Garden*, published anonymously in the same month.

1699 First performance of *The Constant Couple; or, a Trip to the Jubilee* (published 1700) at Drury Lane in November. Credited with the 'discovery' of Anne Oldfield, who created the role of Silvia in *The Recruiting Officer*, in the Mitre tavern.

1700 Contributed to a published collection of *Familiar and Courtly Letters*.

1701 *Sir Harry Wildair*, the unsuccessful sequel to *The Constant Couple*, performed at Drury Lane in April, and published. Contributed to *Letters of Wit, Politicks, and Morality*.

1702 His adaptation of Fletcher's *The Wild Goose Chase* as *The Inconstant* (published 1702) performed at Drury Lane without much success, just before the closing of the theatres for six weeks following the death of William III in March. The satirical comedy *The Twin-Rivals* (published 1703) followed in December, also at Drury Lane, and was an even more pronounced failure. His miscellany of occasional verse and letters, *Love and Business*, published, including the epistolary *'Discourse upon Comedy'*.

1703 Marriage to Margaret Pemell, a widow with three children, whose poverty apparently surprised him. The short farce *The Stage-Coach* (published 1704), adapted from the French, performed at Lincoln's Inn Fields in December, or January 1704, and became an extremely popular afterpiece.

1704 Commissioned as a Lieutenant of Grenadiers, securing him a small but reliable income of £54 a year. Received almost £100 from a Dublin benefit performance of *The Constant Couple*. Birth of his first daughter, Anne Marguerite.

1705 On recruiting service in Lichfield and Shrewsbury. Birth of his second daughter, Mary.

1706 *The Recruiting Officer* (set in Shrewsbury) performed successfully at Drury Lane in April and published. Well received, but Farquhar was already ill, presumably with tuberculosis, and may have sold his commission to raise money.

1707 *The Beaux' Stratagem* (set in Lichfield) performed at the new theatre in the Haymarket in March, and published. But Farquhar was now gravely ill, and he died in a 'back garret' in St. Martin's Lane in April or May, in his thirtieth year. The funeral was paid for by Wilks, to whom Farquhar entrusted the care of his 'two helpless girls'. Posthumous publication of the unauthorized *Love's Catechism* (largely derived from *The Beaux' Stratagem*) and of the heroic poem *Barcellona*.

CHRONOLOGY COMPILED BY SIMON TRUSSLER

COMING NEXT

IN THE MAIN HOUSE   730 1745

Sunday September 10th
The Downshire Players of London
Associate Orchestra at the Royal Court Theatre present

A CONCERT OF MUSIC BY SCARLATTI AND HANDEL

Harpsicord: David Wray Soprano: Rosa Mannion

From October 6
The Royal Court Theatre and Diana Bliss present

APPLES

The Musical by Ian Dury   Directed by Simon Curtis

APPLES is Ian Dury's first musical. It is a vision of contemporary life seen through the eyes of Byline Brown, a tabloid journalist. Brown is on the trail of a major scandal in high places which involves drop outs, low lives and a sinister minister.

IN THE THEATRE UPSTAIRS 730 2554

August 24 — September 16
The Royal Court Theatre in association with Issac Davidov present

BLOOD

by Harwant S. Bains   Directed by Lindsay Posner

BLOOD begins amidst the horrific carnage of the Indian Partition of 1947. It follows the journey of two young sikhs from their small, rural community in the Punjab to the Britain of the 1960's. There they find lucrative work, but also an increasing sense of dislocation.

September 27 — October 21
The Royal Court Theatre presents the Warehouse Theatre, Croydon, production of

THE ASTRONOMER'S GARDEN

by Kevin Hood   Directed by Ted Craig

The Royal Observatory, in 1717, is the setting for this exploration of dangerous passions and obsessive desires.
Flamsteed, the Astronomer Royal, surrounded by his frustrated wife, an unscrupulous maid and an ambitious assistant, jealously attempts to guard his discoveries with the arrival in Greenwich of his arch enemy and eventual successor, Edward Halley.

November 15 December 9
The Warehouse Theatre, Croydon, and the Royal Court Theatre present

SLEEPING NIGHTIE

by Victoria Hardie

The play explores the themes of motherhood, child abuse and male violence and their effect on present and future generations. A lover is discovered through the eye of a camera; dark secrets are revealed in the bright light of a video show...

THE OLIVIER APPEAL
Patron: Lord Olivier

The Appeal was launched in June 1988 — The Royal Court's 100th anniversary year. The target is £800,000 to repair and refurbish the theatre and to enable the English Stage Company to maintain and continue its worldwide reputation as Britain's 'National Theatre of new writing'.

The Royal Court would like to thank the following for their generous contributions to the Appeal:

Jeffrey Archer
Edgar Astaire
Associated British Foods
Andrew Bainbridge
The Clifford Barclay Trust
Phyllis Blackburn
The Elaine and Neville Blond
Charitable Trust
Paul Brooke
Isador Caplan
Peter Carter
Geoffrey Chater
Graham Cowley
David Crosner
The Douglas Heath Eves Trust
Douglas Fairbanks
The Economist
The Esmee Fairbairn Trust
Matthew Evans
Evans and Reiss
Robert Fleming Bank
D J Freeman & Company
Brian Friel
Michael Frayn
Gala (100th Anniversary)
The Godinton Trust
Caroline Goodall
Lord Goodman
Roger Graef
Christopher Hampton
Hatter (IMO) Foundation

The Hedley Trust
Claude Hug
Mr. & Mrs. Trevor John
The John Lewis Partnership
The Kobler Trust
The London and Edinburgh Trust
The Mercers
National Westminster Bank
Anna Louise Neuberg Trust
Olivier Banquet
A.J.G. Patenall
Pirelli Ltd.
A.J.R. Purssell
Mr. & Mrs. J.A. Pye's
Charitable Settlement
St. Quentin Ltd.
The Rayne Foundation
The Lord Sainsbury Trust
Save & Prosper Group
Paul Schofield
Andrew Sinclair
D. R. Slack
W.H. Smith & Son
The Spencer-Wills Trust
Max Stafford-Clark
'Stormy Monday' Charity Premiere
Mary Trevelyan
Andrew Wadsworth
Womens Playhouse Trust
Sandra Yarwood

THE ROYAL COURT THEATRE SOCIETY

For many years now Members of the Royal Court Theatre Society have received special notice of new productions, but why not become a **Friend, Associate** or a **Patron of the Royal Court**, thereby involving yourself directly in maintaining the high standard and unique quality of Royal Court productions — while enjoying complimentary tickets to the shows themselves? Subscriptions run for one year; to become a Member costs £10, a Friend £50 (joint)/£35 (single), an Associate £350, a Patron £1,000.

PATRONS

Jeffrey Archer, Diana Bliss, Caryl Churchill, Issac Davidov, Alfred Davis, Mr. & Mrs. Nicholas Egon, Mrs. Henny Gestetner, Lady Eileen Joseph, Henry Kaye, Tracey Ullman, Julian Wadham.

ASSOCIATES

Peter Boizot, David Capelli, Michael Codron, Jeremy Conway, Stephen Fry, Elizabeth Garvie, The Earl of Gowrie, David Hart, London Arts Discovery Tours, Patricia Marmont, Barbara Minto, Greville Poke, Michael Serlin, Sir Dermot de Trafford, Nick Hern Books, Richard Wilson.

FRIENDS

Paul Adams, Roger Allam & Susan Todd, Robin Anderson, Jane Annakin, John Arthur, Mrs. M. Bagust, Martine Baker, Linda Bassett, Paul Bater, Josephine Beddoe, Laura Birkett, Anthony Blond, Bob Boas, Irving H. Brecker, Katie Bradford, Jim Broadbent, Alan Brodie, Ralph Brown, A.J.H. Buckley, Stuart Burge, Nell Goodhue Cady, Laurence Cann, Susan Card, Guy Chapman, Steve Childs, Ruby Cohn, Angela Coles, Sandra Cook, Lynn & Bernhard Cottrell, Lou Coulson, Peter Cregeen, Harriet Cruickshank, B. R. Cuzner, Mrs. Der Pao Graham, Anne Devlin, Mrs. V.A. Dimant, Julia Dos Santos, R.H. & B.H. Dowler, Adrian Charles Dunbar, Susan Dunnett, Pamela Edwardes, George A. Elliott III, Jan Evans, Trevor Eve, Kenneth Ewing, Leonard Fenton, Mr. & Mrs. Thomas Fenton, Kate Feast, M.H. Flash, Robert Fox, Gilly Fraser, David Gant, Kerry Gardner, Anne Garwood, Sarah Garner, Alfred Molina & Jill Gascoine, Jonathan Gems, Frank & Woji Gero, Beth Goddard, Lord Goodman, Joan Grahame, Roger Graef, Rod Hall, Sharon Hamper, Shahab Hanif, A.M. Harrison, Vivien Heilbron, Jan Harvey, Peter Headill, Sarah Hellings, Jocelyn Herbert, Ashley & Pauline Hill, David Horovitch, Dusty Hughes, Vi Hughes, Diana Hull, Susan Imhof, Trevor Ingman, Kenny Ireland, Jonathan Isaacs, Alison E. Jackson, Richard Jackson, Dick Jarrett, B. E. Jenkins, Hugh Jenkins, Dominic Jephcott, Paul Jesson, Donald Jones, Dr. & Mrs. David Josefowitz, Elizabeth Karr Tashman, Sharon Kean, Alice Kennelly, Jean Knox, Sir Kerry & Lady St. Johnston, Mrs. O. Lahr, Dr. R.J. Lande, Iain Lanyon, Hugh Laurie, Alison Leathart, Peter Ledeboer, Sheila Lemon, Peter L. Levy, Robert S. Linton, Mr & Mrs M. M. Littman, Roger & Moira Lubbock, John & Erica Macdonald, Suzie Mackenzie, Marina Mahler, Paul Mari, Rosy Nasreen & Dr. Conal Liam Mannion, Marina Martin, Patricia Marx, Anna Massey, S. A. Mason, Paul Matthews, Elaine Maycock, Philip L. McDonald, Ian McMillan, James Midgley, Louise Miller, Anthony Minghella, L.A.G. Morris, T. Murnaghan, Alex Nash, Linda Newns, Sally Newton, John Nicholls, Michael Nyman, Nick Marston, Richard O'Brien, Eileen & John O'Keefe, Donal O'Leary, Stephen Oliver, Gary Olsen, Mark Padmore, Norma Papp, Alan David & Jane Penrose, Ronald Pickup, Pauline Pinder, Harold Pinter, Nigel Planer, Laura Plumb, Peter Polkinghorne, Trevor Preston, R. Puttick, Margaret Ramsay, Jane Rayne, B.J. & Rosmarie Reynolds, E.W. Richards, Alan Rickman, David Robb, Martin & Jennifer Roddy, Christie Ryan, George Scheider, Rosemary Squire, A.J. Sayers, Leah Schmidt, Martin & Glynis Scurr, Jennifer Sebag-Montefiore, Mrs. L.M. Sieff, Paul Sinclair Brooke, Andrew Sinclair and Sonia Melchett, Ms. A.M. Jamieson & Mr. A.P. Smith, Peter A. Smith, Jane Snowden, Max Stafford-Clark, Louise Stein, Jenny Stein, Jeff Steitzer, Lindsay Stevens, Pearl Stewart, Richard Stokes, Richard Stone, Rob Sutherland, Dudley Sutton, Audrey & Gordon Taylor, Steve Tedbury, Nigel Terry, Mary Trevelyan, Amanda and R. L. W. Triggs, Elizabeth Troop, Mrs. Anne Underwood, Kiomars Vejdani, Maureen Vincent, Karen and Wes Wadman, Andrew Wadsworth, Harriet Walter, Julie Walters, Tim Watson, Nicholas Wright, Charles & Victoria Wright.

FOR THE ROYAL COURT

DIRECTION

Artistic Director.. MAX STAFFORD-CLARK
Deputy Director .... SIMON CURTIS
Casting Director ....LISA MAKIN
Literary Manager..KATE HARWOOD
Assistant Director..PHILIP HOWARD
Artistic Assistant .... MELANIE KENYON
Arts Council Writer in Residence..CLARE McINTYRE

PRODUCTION

Production Manager ....BO BARTON
Chief Electrician ....COLIN ROXBOROUGH
Deputy Chief Electrician ....JAMES ARMSTRONG
Electrician .... DENIS O'HARE*
Sound Designer.. BRYAN BOWEN
Board Operators..STEVE HEPWORTH*
Master Carpenter .... CHRIS BAGUST
Deputy Master Carpenter..ALAN JOYCE
Wardrobe Supervisor .... JENNIFER COOK
Deputy Wardrobe Supervisor...CATHIE SKILBECK

ADMINISTRATION

General Manager ....GRAHAM COWLEY
Assistant to General Manager.. LUCY WOOLLATT
Finance Administrator.. STEPHEN MORRIS
Finance Assistant .... RACHEL HARRISON
Press (730 2652)..TAMSIN THOMAS
Marketing & Publicity Manager .... GUY CHAPMAN
Development Director...TOM PETZAL
Development Assistant .... JACQUELINE VIEIRA
House Manager..WILLIAM DAY
Deputy House Manager ....ALISON SMITH
Bookshop..ANGELA TOULMIN*
Box Office Manager...GILL RUSSELL
Box Office Assistants... GERALD BROOKING, RITA SHARMA
Stage Door/Telephonists .... ANGELA TOULMIN, JAN NOYCE*
Evening Stage Door ....TYRONE LUCAS*
Maintenance...JOHN LORRIGIO
Cleaners...EILEEN CHAPMAN*, IVY JONES*
Firemen ....PAUL KLEINMANN*, DAVID WYATT*

YOUNG PEOPLE'S THEATRE

Director .... ELYSE DODGSON
Administrator ....DOMINIC TICKELL
Youth and Community Worker .... EUTON DALY

*Part-time staff

COUNCIL: Chairman: MATTHEW EVANS, CHRIS BAGUST, BO BARTON, STUART BURGE, ANTHONY C. BURTON, CARYL CHURCHILL, BRIAN COX, HARRIET CRUICKSHANK, SIMON CURTIS, ALLAN DAVIS, DAVID LLOYD DAVIS, ROBERT FOX, MRS. HENNY GESTETNER OBE, DEREK GRANGER, DAVID HARE, JOCELYN HERBERT, DAVID KLEEMAN, HANIF KUREISHI, SONIA MELCHETT, JAMES MIDGLEY, JOAN PLOWRIGHT CBE, GREVILLE POKE, RICHARD PULFORD, JANE RAYNE, JIM TANNER, SIR HUGH WILLATT.

This Theatre is associated with the Regional Theatre Young Directors Scheme.

THE
Recruiting Officer.

A
COMEDY.

As it is Acted at the

THEATRE ROYAL

IN

DRURY-LANE,

By Her MAJESTY's Servants.

Written by Mr. FARQUHAR.

—— *Captique Æolis, donisque coacti.*
Virg. Lib. II. Æneid.

LONDON:

Printed for BERNARD LINTOTT at the *Cross Keys* next
Nando's Coffee-House near *Temple-Bar.*

Price 1 *s.* 6 *d.*

EPISTLE DEDICATORY
To All Friends Round the Wrekin

My Lords and Gentlemen,
  Instead of the mercenary expectations that attend addresses
of this nature, I humbly beg, that this may be received as an
acknowledgment for the favours you have already conferred.
I have transgressed the rules of dedication in offering you   5
anything in that style without first asking your leave; but the
entertainment I found in Shropshire commands me to be
grateful, and that's all I intend.
  'Twas my good fortune to be ordered some time ago into the
place which is made the scene of this comedy; I was a perfect   10
stranger to everything in Salop, but its character of loyalty, the
number of its inhabitants, the alacrity of the gentlemen in
recruiting the army, with their generous and hospitable
reception of strangers.
  This character I found so amply verified in every particular,   15
that you made recruiting, which is the greatest fatigue upon
earth to others, to be the greatest pleasure in the world to me.
  The kingdom cannot show better bodies of men, better
inclinations for the service, more generosity, more good understanding, nor more politeness, than is to be found at the foot of   20
the Wrekin.
  Some little turns of humour that I met with almost within
the shade of that famous hill gave the rise to this comedy; and
people were apprehensive, that, by the example of some others,
I would make the town merry at the expense of the country   25
gentlemen. But they forgot that I was to write a comedy, not a
libel; and that whilst I held to nature, no person of any
character in your country could suffer by being exposed. I have
drawn the justice and the clown in their *puris naturalibus*: the
one an apprehensive, sturdy, brave blockhead; and the other a   30
worthy, honest, generous gentleman, hearty in his country's
cause, and of as good an understanding as I could give him,
which I must confess is far short of his own.
  I humbly beg leave to interline a word or two of the adven-

tures of *The Recruiting Officer* upon the stage. Mr Rich, who   35
commands the company for which those recruits were raised,
has desired me to acquit him before the world of a charge
which he thinks lies heavy upon him for acting this play on
Mr Durfey's third night.

Be it known unto all men by these presents, that it was my   40
act and deed, or rather Mr Durfey's; for he *would* play his third
night against the first of mine. He brought down a huge flight
of frightful birds upon me, when, heaven knows, I had not a
feathered fowl in my play except one single Kite; but I
presently made Plume a bird, because of his name, and Brazen   45
another, because of the feather in his hat; and with these three
I engaged his whole empire, which I think was as great a *wonder*
as any *in the sun*.

But to answer his complaints more gravely, the season was
far advanced; the officers that made the greatest figures in my   50
play were all commanded to their posts abroad, and waited only
for a wind, which might possibly turn in less time than a day;
and I know none of Mr Durfey's birds that had posts abroad
but his woodcocks, and their season is over; so that he might
put off a day with less prejudice than the *Recruiting Officer*   55
could, who has this farther to say for himself, that he was
posted before the other spoke, and could not with credit recede
from his station.

These and some other rubs this comedy met with before it
appeared. But on the other hand, it had powerful helps to set it   60
forward: the Duke of Ormonde encouraged the author, and the
Earl of Orrery approved the play. My recruits were reviewed
by my general and my colonel, and could not fail to pass
muster, and still to add to my success, they were raised among
my friends round the Wrekin.   65

This Health has the advantage over our other celebrated
toasts, never to grow worse for the wearing; 'tis a lasting
beauty, old without age and common without scandal. That
you may live long to set it cheerfully round, and to enjoy the
abundant pleasures of your fair and plentiful country, is the   70
hearty wish of,

My Lords and Gentlemen,
Your most obliged,
and most obedient servant,
Geo. Farquhar.   75

THE PROLOGUE

In ancient times, when Helen's fatal charms
Roused the contending universe to arms,
The Grecian council happily deputes
The sly Ulysses forth – to raise recruits.
The artful captain found, without delay,   5
Where great Achilles, a deserter, lay.
Him Fate had warned to shun the Trojan blows;
Him Greece required – against their Trojan foes.
All the recruiting arts were needful here
To raise this great, this tim'rous volunteer.   10
Ulysses well could talk – he stirs, he warms
The warlike youth. He listens to the charms
Of plunder, fine laced coats, and glitt'ring arms.
Ulysses caught the young aspiring boy,
And listed him who wrought the fate of Troy.   15
Thus by recruiting was bold Hector slain;
Recruiting thus fair Helen did regain.
If for one Helen such prodigious things
Were acted, that they even listed kings;
If for one Helen's artful, vicious charms,   20
Half the transported world was found in arms;
What for so many Helens may we dare,
Whose minds, as well as faces, are so fair?
If, by one Helen's eyes, old Greece could find
Its Homer fired to write – even Homer blind,   25
The Britons sure beyond compare may write,
That view so many Helens every night.

THE RECRUITING OFFICER

Act I, Scene i

The Market-place
DRUMMER *beats the 'Grenadier March'*
Enter SERGEANT KITE, *followed by the* MOB

KITE (*Making a speech*)
If any gentlemen soldiers, or others, have a mind to serve
Her Majesty, and pull down the French king; if any prentices
have severe masters, any children have undutiful parents; if
any servants have too little wages, or any husband too much
wife; let them repair to the noble Sergeant Kite, at the Sign   5
of the Raven, in this good town of Shrewsbury, and they shall
receive present relief and entertainment. – Gentlemen, I
don't beat my drums here to ensnare or inveigle any man;
for you must know, gentlemen, that I am a man of honour.
Besides, I don't beat up for common soldiers; no, I list only   10
grenadiers, grenadiers, gentlemen – pray, gentlemen, observe
this cap – this is the cap of honour, it dubs a man a gentleman in the drawing of a tricker; and he that has the good
fortune to be born six foot high was born to be a great man.
(*To one of the Mob*) Sir, will you give me leave to try this cap   15
upon your head?
MOB
Is there no harm in't? Won't the cap list me?
KITE
No, no, no more than I can, – come, let me see how it
becomes you.
MOB
Are you sure there be no conjuration in it, no gunpowder   20
plot upon me?
KITE
No, no, friend; don't fear, man.
MOB
My mind misgives me plaguily – let me see it. (*Going to put
it on*) It smells woundily of sweat and brimstone; pray,
Sergeant, what writing is this upon the face of it?   25
KITE
'The Crown, or the Bed of Honour'.

MOB

Pray now, what may be that same bed of honour?

KITE

Oh, a mighty large bed, bigger by half than the great bed of
Ware, ten thousand people may lie in't together and never
feel one another.   30

MOB

My wife and I would do well to lie in't, for we don't care for
feeling one another – but do folk sleep sound in this same bed
of honour?

KITE

Sound! Aye, so sound that they never wake.

MOB

Wauns! I wish again that my wife lay there.   35

KITE

Say you so? Then I find, brother –

MOB

Brother! Hold there, friend, I'm no kindred to you that I
know of, as yet – look'ee, Sergeant, no coaxing, no wheedling,
d'ye see; if I have a mind to list, why so – if not, why 'tis not
so – therefore take your cap and your brothership back   40
again, for I an't disposed at this present writing – no
coaxing, no brothering me, faith.

KITE

I coax! I wheedle! I'm above it. Sir, I have served twenty
campaigns. But sir, you talk well, and I must own that you
are a man every inch of you, a pretty, young, sprightly   45
fellow – I love a fellow with a spirit, but I scorn to coax, 'tis
base; though I must say that never in my life have I seen a
man better built; how firm and strong he treads, he steps
like a castle! But I scorn to wheedle any man – come,
honest lad, will you take share of a pot?   50

MOB

Nay, for that matter, I'll spend my penny with the best he
that wears a head, that is, begging your pardon, sir, and in
a fair way.

KITE

Give me your hand then; and now, gentlemen, I have no
more to say but this – here's a purse of gold, and there is a   55
tub of humming ale at my quarters; 'tis the Queen's money
and the Queen's drink. She's a generous queen and loves
her subjects – I hope, gentlemen, you won't refuse the
Queen's health?

ALL MOB

No, no, no.   60

KITE

Huzza then! Huzza for the Queen, and the honour of
Shropshire!

ALL MOB

Huzza!

KITE

Beat drum.

Exeunt, drummer beating the 'Grenadier March'

Enter PLUME *in a riding habit*

PLUME

By the Grenadier March that should be my drum, and by that   65
shout it should beat with success – let me see – (*looks on his
watch*) – four o'clock – at ten yesterday morning I left
London – a hundred and twenty miles in thirty hours is
pretty smart riding, but nothing to the fatigue of recruiting.

Enter KITE

KITE

Welcome to Shrewsbury, noble Captain: from the banks of   70
the Danube to the Severn side, noble Captain, you're
welcome.

PLUME

A very elegant reception indeed, Mr Kite, I find you are
fairly entered into your recruiting strain – pray, what
success?   75

KITE

I have been here but a week and I have recruited five.

PLUME

Five! Pray, what are they?

KITE

I have listed the strong man of Kent, the king of the gypsies,
a Scotch pedlar, a scoundrel attorney, and a Welsh parson.

PLUME

An attorney! Wert thou mad? List a lawyer! Discharge him,   80
discharge him this minute.

KITE

Why, sir?

PLUME

Because I will have nobody in my company that can write;
a fellow that can write, can draw petitions – I say, this
minute discharge him.   85

KITE

And what shall I do with the parson?

PLUME

Can he write?

KITE

Umh – he plays rarely upon the fiddle.

PLUME

Keep him by all means. But how stands the country affected?
Were the people pleased with the news of my coming to   90
town?

KITE

Sir, the mob are so pleased with your honour, and the
justices and better sort of people are so delighted with me,
that we shall soon do our business. But, sir, you have got a
recruit here that you little think of.   95

PLUME

Who?

KITE

One that you beat up for last time you were in the country:
You remember your old friend Molly at the Castle?

PLUME

She's not with child, I hope.

KITE

No, no, sir; she was brought to bed yesterday.   100

PLUME

Kite, you must father the child.

KITE

Humph – and so her friends will oblige me to marry the
mother.

PLUME

If they should, we'll take her with us, she can wash, you
know, and make a bed upon occasion.   105

KITE

Aye, or unmake it upon occasion. But your honour knows
that I'm married already.

PLUME

To how many?

KITE

I can't tell readily – I have set them down here upon the back
of the muster-roll. (*Draws it out*) Let me see – *Imprimis*, 110
Mrs Sheely Snickereyes, she sells potatoes upon Ormonde
Quay in Dublin – Peggy Guzzle, the brandy-woman at the
Horse-guard at Whitehall – Dolly Waggon, the carrier's
daughter in Hull – Mademoiselle Van-bottom-flat at the

Buss – then Jenny Oakum, the ship-carpenter's widow at   115
Portsmouth; but I don't reckon upon her, for she was
married at the same time to two lieutenants of marines, and
a man of war's boatswain.

PLUME

A full company – you have named five – come, make 'em half
a dozen, Kite. Is the child a boy or a girl?   120

KITE

A chopping boy.

PLUME

Then set the mother down in your list, and the boy in mine;
enter him a grenadier by the name of Francis Kite, absent
upon furlough – I'll allow you a man's pay for his subsistence; and now go comfort the wench in the straw.   125

KITE

I shall, sir.

PLUME

But hold, have you made any use of your German doctor's
habit since you arrived?

KITE

Yes, yes, sir; and my fame's all about the country for the
most faithful fortune-teller that ever told a lie; I was obliged   130
to let my landlord into the secret for the convenience of
keeping it so, but he's an honest fellow and will be trusty to
any roguery that is confided to him. This device, sir, will get
you men, and me money, which I think is all we want at
present – but yonder comes your friend Mr Worthy – has   135
your honour any farther commands?

PLUME

None at present.   *Exit* KITE

'Tis indeed the picture of Worthy, but the life's departed.

Enter WORTHY

PLUME

What, arms a-cross, Worthy! Methinks you should hold 'em
open when a friend's so near. The man has got the vapours   140
in his ears, I believe; I must expel this melancholy spirit.
      Spleen, thou worst of fiends below,
      Fly, I conjure thee by this magic blow.
            Slaps WORTHY *on the shoulder*

WORTHY

Plume! My dear Captain, welcome. Safe and sound returned!

PLUME

I 'scaped safe from Germany, and sound, I hope, from   145

London: you see I have lost neither leg, arm nor nose; then for my inside, 'tis neither troubled with sympathies nor antipathies, and I have an excellent stomach for roast beef.

WORTHY
Thou art a happy fellow; once I was so.

PLUME
What ails thee, man? No inundations nor earthquakes in   150
Wales, I hope? Has your father rose from the dead, and reassumed his estate?

WORTHY
No.

PLUME
Then you are married, surely.

WORTHY
No.   155

PLUME
Then you are mad, or turning Quaker.

WORTHY
Come, I must out with it – your once gay, roving friend is dwindled into an obsequious, thoughtful, romantic, constant coxcomb.

PLUME
And pray, what is all this for?   160

WORTHY
For a woman.

PLUME
Shake hands, brother, if you go to that – behold me as obsequious, as thoughtful, and as constant a coxcomb as your worship.

WORTHY
For whom?   165

PLUME
For a regiment. – But for a woman! 'Sdeath! I have been constant to fifteen at a time, but never melancholy for one; and can the love of one bring you into this pickle? Pray, who is this miraculous Helen?

WORTHY
A Helen indeed, not to be won under a ten years' siege; as   170
great a beauty, and as great a jilt.

PLUME
A jilt! Pho! Is she as great a whore?

WORTHY
No, no.

PLUME

'Tis ten thousand pities; but who is she? Do I know her?

WORTHY

Very well.   175

PLUME

Impossible! – I know no woman that will hold out a ten
years' siege.

WORTHY

What think you of Melinda?

PLUME

Melinda! Why, she began to capitulate this time twelve-
month, and offered to surrender upon honourable terms;   180
and I advised you to propose a settlement of five hundred
pound a year to her, before I went last abroad.

WORTHY

I did, and she hearkened to't, desiring only one week to
consider; when beyond her hopes the town was relieved, and
I forced to turn my siege into a blockade.   185

PLUME

Explain, explain.

WORTHY

My Lady Richly, her aunt in Flintshire, dies, and leaves her
at this critical time twenty thousand pound.

PLUME

Oh, the devil! What a delicate woman was there spoiled! But
by the rules of war now, Worthy, blockade was foolish –   190
after such a convoy of provisions was entered the place, you
could have no thought of reducing it by famine – you should
have redoubled your attacks, taken the town by storm, or
have died upon the breach.

WORTHY

I did make one general assault, and pushed it with all my   195
forces; but I was so vigorously repulsed, that despairing of
ever gaining her for a mistress, I have altered my conduct,
given my addresses the obsequious and distant turn, and
court her now for a wife.

PLUME

So, as you grew obsequious, she grew haughty, and because 200
you approached her as a goddess, she used you like a dog.

WORTHY

Exactly.

PLUME

'Tis the way of 'em all. Come, Worthy, your obsequious and
distant airs will never bring you together; you must not think

to surmount her pride by your humility. Would you bring   205
her to better thoughts of you, she must be reduced to a
meaner opinion of herself – let me see – the very first thing
that I would do, should be to lie with her chambermaid, and
hire three or four wenches in the neighbourhood to report
that I had got them with child. Suppose we lampooned all   210
the pretty women in town, and left her out? Or what if we
made a ball, and forgot to invite her, with one or two of the
ugliest?

WORTHY
These would be mortifications, I must confess; but we live in
such a precise, dull place that we can have no balls, no   215
lampoons, no –

PLUME
What! No bastards! And so many recruiting officers in
town; I thought 'twas a maxim among them to leave as many
recruits in the country as they carried out.

WORTHY
Nobody doubts your goodwill, noble Captain, in serving your   220
country with your best blood: witness our friend Molly at
the Castle, – there have been tears in town about that
business, Captain.

PLUME
I hope Silvia has not heard of't.

WORTHY
Oh sir, have you thought of her? I began to fancy you had   225
forgot poor Silvia.

PLUME
Your affairs had put mine quite out of my head. 'Tis true,
Silvia and I had once agreed to go to bed together, could we
have adjusted preliminaries; but she would have the
wedding before consummation, and I was for consum-   230
mation before the wedding – we could not agree. She was a
pert obstinate fool, and would lose her maidenhead her own
way, so she may keep it for Plume.

WORTHY
But do you intend to marry upon no other conditions?

PLUME
Your pardon, sir, I'll marry upon no condition at all, – if I   235
should, I'm resolved never to bind myself to a woman for my
whole life, till I know whether I shall like her company for
half an hour. Suppose I married a woman that wanted a leg?
Such a thing might be, unless I examined the goods beforehand. If people would but try one another's constitutions   240

before they engaged, it would prevent all these elopements,
divorces, and the devil knows what.

WORTHY

Nay, for that matter, the town did not stick to say, that –

PLUME

I hate country towns for that reason – if your town has a
dishonourable thought of Silvia, it deserves to be burnt to   245
the ground. – I love Silvia, I admire her frank, generous
disposition; there's something in that girl more than woman,
her sex is but a foil to her – the ingratitude, dissimulation,
envy, pride, avarice, and vanity of her sister females, do but
set off their contraries in her – in short, were I once a   250
general, I would marry her.

WORTHY

Faith, you have reason; for were you but a corporal, she
would marry you. But my Melinda coquettes it with every
fellow she sees – I lay fifty pound she makes love to you.

PLUME

I'll lay fifty pound that I return it if she does – look'ee,   255
Worthy, I'll win her and give her to you afterwards.

WORTHY

If you win her you shall wear her, faith; I would not give a
fig for the conquest without the credit of the victory.

Enter KITE

KITE

Captain, Captain, a word in your ear.

PLUME

You may speak out, here are none but friends.   260

KITE

You know, sir, that you sent me to comfort the good woman
in the straw, Mrs Molly – my wife, Mr Worthy.

WORTHY

Oho! Very well – I wish you joy, Mr Kite.

KITE

Your worship very well may – for I have got both a wife and
a child in half an hour – but as I was a-saying, you sent me   265
to comfort Mrs Molly – my wife, I mean – but what d'ye
think, sir? She was better comforted before I came.

PLUME

As how?

KITE

Why, sir, a footman in a blue livery had brought her ten
guineas to buy her baby clothes.   270

PLUME
Who in the name of wonder could send them?

KITE
Nay, sir, I must whisper that – (*Whispers*) Mrs Silvia.

PLUME
Silvia! Generous creature.

WORTHY
Silvia! Impossible.

KITE
Here be the guineas, sir; I took the gold as part of my wife's   275
portion. Nay, farther, sir, she sent word the child should be
taken all imaginable care of, and that she intended to stand
godmother. The same footman, as I was coming to you with
this news, called after me, and told me that his lady would
speak with me – I went, and upon hearing that you were   280
come to town, she gave me half a guinea for the news, and
ordered me to tell you, that Justice Balance, her father, who
is just come out of the country, would be glad to see you.

PLUME
There's a girl for you, Worthy – is there anything of
woman in this? No, 'tis noble and generous, manly friend-   285
ship; show me another woman that would lose an inch of
her prerogative that way, without tears, fits, and reproaches.
The common jealousy of her sex, which is nothing but their
avarice of pleasure, she despises; and can part with the lover,
though she dies for the man. – Come, Worthy, where's the   290
best wine? For there I'll quarter.

WORTHY
Horton has a fresh pipe of choice Barcelona, which I would
not let him pierce before, because I reserved the maidenhead of it for your welcome to town.

PLUME
Let's away then – Mr Kite, wait on the lady with my humble   295
service, and tell her I shall only refresh a little, and wait
upon her.

WORTHY
Hold, Kite – have you seen the other recruiting captain?

KITE
No, sir.

PLUME
Another? Who is he?   300

WORTHY
My rival in the first place, and the most unaccountable
fellow; but I'll tell you more as we go.   *Exeunt*

[Act I], Scene ii

MELINDA'*s Apartment*
MELINDA *and* SILVIA *meeting*

MELINDA

Welcome to town, cousin Silvia. (*Salute*) I envied you your
retreat in the country; for Shrewsbury, methinks, and all
your heads of shires, are the most irregular places for living;
here we have smoke, noise, scandal, affectation, and preten-
sion; in short, everything to give the spleen, and nothing to   5
divert it – then the air is intolerable.

SILVIA

Oh, madam, I have heard the town commended for its air.

MELINDA

But you don't consider, Silvia, how long I have lived in't!
For I can assure you, that to a lady the least nice in her
constitution, no air can be good above half a year; change of   10
air I take to be the most agreeable of any variety in life.

SILVIA

As you say, cousin Melinda, there are several sorts of airs:
airs in conversation, airs in behaviour, airs in dress; then we
have our quality airs, our sickly airs, our reserved airs, and
sometimes our impudent airs.   15

MELINDA

Psha! I talk only of the air we breathe or more properly of
that we taste – have not you, Silvia, found a vast difference in
the taste of airs?

SILVIA

Pray, cousin, are not vapours a sort of air? Taste air! You
might as well tell me I may feed on air. But prithee, my dear   20
Melinda, don't put on such an air to me; your education and
mine were just the same, and I remember the time when we
never troubled our heads about air, but when the sharp air
from the Welsh mountains made our noses drop in a cold
morning at the boarding-school.   25

MELINDA

Our education, cousin, was the same, but our temperaments
had nothing alike; you have the constitution of a horse –

SILVIA

So far as to be troubled with neither spleen, colic, nor
vapours; I need no salt for my stomach, no hartshorn for my
head, nor wash for my complexion; I can gallop all the   30
morning after the hunting-horn, and all the evening after a

fiddle. In short, I can do everything with my father but drink
and shoot flying; and I'm sure I can do everything my
mother could, were I put to the trial.

MELINDA

You're in a fair way of being put to't; for I'm told your   35
captain is come to town.

SILVIA

Aye, Melinda, he is come, and I'll take care he shan't go
without a companion.

MELINDA

You're certainly mad, cousin.

SILVIA

And there's a pleasure, sure, in being mad,   40
Which none but madmen know.

MELINDA

Thou poor, romantic Quixote, hast thou the vanity to
imagine that a young, sprightly officer that rambles o'er half
the globe in half a year, can confine his thoughts to the little
daughter of a country justice in an obscure corner of the   45
world?

SILVIA

Pshaw! What care I for his thoughts? I should not like a man
with confined thoughts, it shows a narrowness of soul.
Constancy is but a dull, sleepy quality at best, they will
hardly admit it among the manly virtues; nor do I think it   50
deserves a place with bravery, knowledge, policy, justice, and
some other qualities that are proper to that noble sex. In
short, Melinda, I think a petticoat a mighty simple thing,
and I'm heartily tired of my sex.

MELINDA

That is, you are tired of an appendix to our sex, that you   55
can't so handsomely get rid of in petticoats as if you were in
breeches. O'my conscience, Silvia, hadst thou been a man,
thou hadst been the greatest rake in Christendom.

SILVIA

I should endeavour to know the world, which a man can
never do thoroughly without half a hundred friendships, and   60
as many amours. But now I think on't, how stands your
affair with Mr Worthy?

MELINDA

He's my aversion.

SILVIA

Vapours!

MELINDA

What do you say, madam?   65

SILVIA

I say that you should not use that honest fellow so in-
humanely. He's a gentleman of parts and fortune, and beside
that he's my Plume's friend, and by all that's sacred, if you
don't use him better, I shall expect satisfaction.

MELINDA

Satisfaction! You begin to fancy yourself in breeches in good   70
earnest. But to be plain with you, I like Worthy the worse for
being so intimate with your captain, for I take him to be a
loose, idle, unmannerly coxcomb.

SILVIA

Oh, madam! You never saw him, perhaps, since you were
mistress of twenty thousand pound; you only knew him when   75
you were capitulating with Worthy for a settlement, which
perhaps might encourage him to be a little loose and unmannerly with you.

MELINDA

What do you mean, madam?

SILVIA

My meaning needs no interpretation, madam.   80

MELINDA

Better it had, madam, for methinks you're too plain.

SILVIA

If you mean the plainness of my person, I think your ladyship as plain as me to the full.

MELINDA

Were I assured of that, I should be glad to take up with a
rakehelly officer as you do.   85

SILVIA

Again! Look'ee, madam – you're in your own house.

MELINDA

And if you had kept in yours, I should have excused you.

SILVIA

Don't be troubled, madam, I shan't desire to have my visit
returned.

MELINDA

The sooner therefore you make an end of this the better.   90

SILVIA

I'm easily advised to follow my inclinations – so, madam –
your humble servant.   *Exit*

MELINDA

Saucy thing!

Enter LUCY

LUCY

What's the matter, madam?

MELINDA

Did you not see the proud nothing, how she swells upon the   95
arrival of her fellow?

LUCY

Her fellow has not been long enough arrived to occasion any
great swelling, madam; I don't believe she has seen him yet.

MELINDA

Nor shan't if I can help it; let me see – I have it – bring me
pen and ink – hold, I'll go write in my closet.   100

LUCY

An answer to this letter, I hope, madam. (*Presents a letter*)

MELINDA

Who sent it?

LUCY

Your captain, madam.

MELINDA

He's a fool, and I'm tired of him, send it back unopened.

LUCY

The messenger's gone, madam.   105

MELINDA

Then how shall I send an answer? Call him back immediately, while I go write.   *Exeunt*

Act II, Scene i

An Apartment [*in* JUSTICE BALANCE's *House*]
Enter JUSTICE BALANCE *and* PLUME

BALANCE

Look'ee, Captain, give us but blood for our money, and you
shan't want men. I remember that for some years of the last
war we had no blood nor wounds but in the officers' mouths,
nothing for our millions but newspapers not worth a reading
– our armies did nothing but play at prison bars and hide-   5
and-seek with the enemy; but now ye have brought us
colours and standards and prisoners; odsmylife, Captain, get
us but another Marshal of France, and I'll go myself for a
soldier.

PLUME

Pray, Mr Balance, how does your fair daughter?   10

BALANCE
Ah, Captain, what is my daughter to a Marshal of France?
We're upon a nobler subject. I want to have a particular
description of the Battle of Höchstädt.

PLUME
The battle, sir, was a very pretty battle as one should desire to
see, but we were all so intent upon victory that we never   15
minded the battle; all that I know of the matter is, our
general commanded us to beat the French, and we did so,
and if he pleases to say the word, we'll do't again. – But pray,
sir, how does Mrs Silvia?

BALANCE
Still upon Silvia! For shame, Captain – you're engaged   20
already, wedded to the war; victory is your mistress, and it
is below a soldier to think of any other.

PLUME
As a mistress, I confess, but as a friend, Mr Balance.

BALANCE
Come, come, Captain, never mince the matter, would not
you debauch my daughter if you could?   25

PLUME
How, sir! I hope she's not to be debauched.

BALANCE
Faith, but she is, sir, and any woman in England of her age
and complexion, by a man of your youth and vigour. Look'ee,
Captain, once I was young and once an officer as you are, and
I can guess at your thoughts now by what mine were then,   30
and I remember very well, that I would have given one of my
legs to have deluded the daughter of an old, plain country
gentleman, as like me as I was then like you.

PLUME
But, sir, was that country gentleman your friend and
benefactor?   35

BALANCE
Not much of that.

PLUME
There the comparison breaks; the favours, sir, that –

BALANCE
Pho, I hate speeches. If I have done you any service, Captain,
'twas to please myself, for I love thee; and if I could part with
my girl, you should have her as soon as any young fellow I   40
know; I hope you have more honour than to quit the service,
and she more prudence than to follow the camp. But she's
at her own disposal, she has fifteen hundred pound in her

pocket, and so – Silvia, Silvia!   *Calls*

Enter SILVIA

SILVIA

There are some letters, sir, come by the post from London;   45
I left them upon the table in your closet.

BALANCE

And here is a gentleman from Germany. (*Presents* PLUME *to
her*) Captain, you'll excuse me, I'll go read my letters, and
wait on you.   *Exit*

SILVIA

Sir, you're welcome to England.   50

PLUME

You are indebted to me a welcome, madam, since the hopes
of receiving it from this fair hand was the principal cause of
my seeing England.

SILVIA

I have often heard that soldiers were sincere, shall I venture
to believe public report?   55

PLUME

You may, when 'tis backed by private insurance; for I
swear, madam, by the honour of my profession, that what-
ever dangers I went upon, it was with the hope of making
myself more worthy of your esteem, and if I ever had
thoughts of preserving my life, 'twas for the pleasure of   60
dying at your feet.

SILVIA

Well, well, you shall die at my feet, or where you will; but
you know, sir, there is a certain will and testament to be made
beforehand.

PLUME

My will, madam, is made already, and there it is. (*Gives her*   65
a parchment) And if you please to open that parchment,
which was drawn the evening before the Battle of Blenheim,
you will find whom I left my heir.
                              SILVIA *opens the will and reads*

SILVIA

'Mrs Silvia Balance'. – Well, Captain, this is a handsome
and a substantial compliment; but I can assure you I am   70
much better pleased with the bare knowledge of your
intention than I should have been in the possession of your
legacy; but methinks, sir, you should have left something to
your little boy at the Castle.

PLUME

(*Aside*) That's home. – My little boy! Lack-a-day, madam,   75
that alone may convince you 'twas none of mine; why the
girl, madam, is my sergeant's wife, and so the poor creature
gave out that I was father in hopes that my friends might
support her in case of necessity; that was all, madam. – My
boy! No, no, no.   80

Enter SERVANT

SERVANT

Madam, my master has received some ill news from London
and desires to speak with you immediately, and he begs the
captain's pardon that he can't wait on him as he promised.

PLUME

Ill news! Heavens avert it; nothing could touch me nearer
than to see that generous, worthy gentleman afflicted; I'll   85
leave you to comfort him, and be assured that if my life and
fortune can be any way serviceable to the father of my Silvia,
he shall freely command both.

SILVIA

The necessity must be very pressing that would engage me
to endanger either.   *Exeunt severally*   90

[Act II], Scene ii

Another Apartment
Enter BALANCE *and* SILVIA

SILVIA

Whilst there is life there is hope, sir; perhaps my brother may
recover.

BALANCE

We have but little reason to expect it. Dr Kilman acquaints
me here, that before this comes to my hands he fears I shall
have no son. – Poor Owen! But the decree is just; I was   5
pleased with the death of my father, because he left me an
estate, and now I'm punished with the loss of an heir to
inherit mine. I must now look upon you as the only hopes of
my family, and I expect that the augmentation of your
fortune will give you fresh thoughts and new prospects.   10

SILVIA

My desire of being punctual in my obedience requires that
you would be plain in your commands, sir.

BALANCE

The death of your brother makes you sole heiress to my
estate, which you know is about twelve hundred pounds a
year; this fortune gives you a fair claim to quality and a title;   15
you must set a just value upon yourself, and in plain terms
think no more of Captain Plume.

SILVIA

You have often commended the gentleman, sir.

BALANCE

And I do so still; he's a very pretty fellow; but though I
liked him well enough for a bare son-in-law, I don't approve   20
of him for an heir to my estate and family; fifteen hundred
pound, indeed, I might trust in his hands, and it might do
the young fellow a kindness, but odsmylife, twelve hundred
pound a year would ruin him, quite turn his brain. A
captain of foot worth twelve hundred pound a year! 'Tis a   25
prodigy in nature. Besides this, I have five or six thousand
pounds in woods upon my estate; oh, that would make him
stark mad! For you must know that all captains have a
mighty aversion to timber, they can't endure to see trees
standing. Then I should have some rogue of a builder by the   30
help of his damned magic art transform my noble oaks and
elms into cornishes, portals, sashes, birds, beasts, gods, and
devils, to adorn some maggoty, new-fashioned bauble upon
the Thames; and then you should have a dog of a gardener
bring a *habeas corpus* for my *terra firma*, remove it to Chelsea   35
or Twit'nam, and clap it into grass-plats and gravel walks.

Enter a SERVANT

SERVANT

Sir, here's one below with a letter for your worship, but he
will deliver it into no hands but your own.

BALANCE

Come, show me the messenger.   *Exit with* SERVANT

SILVIA

Make the dispute between love and duty, and I am Prince   40
Prettyman exactly. – If my brother dies, ah, poor brother!
If he lives, ah, poor sister! – 'Tis bad both ways; I'll try it
again, – follow my own inclinations and break my father's
heart, or obey his commands and break my own; worse and
worse. Suppose I take it thus – a moderate fortune, a pretty   45
fellow, and a pad; or a fine estate, a coach-and-six, and an
ass – that will never do neither.

Enter BALANCE *and* SERVANT

BALANCE

Put four horses into the coach.

To the SERVANT, *who goes out*

Ho, Silvia –

SILVIA

Sir.   50

BALANCE

How old were you when your mother died?

SILVIA

So young that I don't remember I ever had one; and you
have been so careful, so indulgent to me since, that indeed I
never wanted one.

BALANCE

Have I ever denied you anything you asked of me?   55

SILVIA

Never, that I remember.

BALANCE

Then, Silvia, I must beg that once in your life you would
grant me a favour.

SILVIA

Why should you question it, sir?

BALANCE

I don't, but I would rather counsel than command; I don't   60
propose this with the authority of a parent, but as the advice
of your friend, that you would take the coach this moment
and go into the country.

SILVIA

Does this advice, sir, proceed from the contents of the letter
you received just now?   65

BALANCE

No matter; I will be with you in three or four days and then
give you my reasons. But before you go, I expect you will
make me one solemn promise.

SILVIA

Propose the thing, sir.

BALANCE

That you will never dispose of yourself to any man without   70
my consent.

SILVIA

I promise.

BALANCE

Very well, and to be even with you, I promise I will never

dispose of you without your own consent; and so, Silvia, the
coach is ready; farewell. (*Leads her to the door and returns*)   75
Now she's gone, I'll examine the contents of this letter a
little nearer. (*Reads*)
   Sir,
      My intimacy with Mr Worthy has drawn a secret from
   him that he had from his friend Captain Plume, and my   80
   friendship and relation to your family oblige me to give
   you timely notice of it: the captain has dishonourable
   designs upon my cousin Silvia. Evils of this nature are
   more easily prevented than amended, and that you would
   immediately send my cousin into the country is the advice   85
   of,
                              Sir, your humble servant,
                                    MELINDA.
Why, the devil's in the young fellows of this age; they're ten
times worse than they were in my time! Had he made my   90
daughter a whore and forswore it like a gentleman, I could
have almost pardoned it; but to tell tales beforehand is
monstrous! Hang it, I can fetch down a woodcock or snipe,
and why not a hat and feather? I have a case of good pistols,
and have a good mind to try.   95

                    Enter WORTHY

BALANCE
Worthy, your servant.
WORTHY
I'm sorry, sir, to be the messenger of ill news.
BALANCE
I apprehend it, sir; you have heard that my son Owen is past
recovery.
WORTHY
My advices say he's dead, sir.   100
BALANCE
He's happy, and I am satisfied; the strokes of heaven I can
bear; but injuries from men, Mr Worthy, are not so easily
supported.
WORTHY
I hope, sir, you're under no apprehension of wrong from
anybody?   105
BALANCE
You know I ought to be.
WORTHY
You wrong my honour, sir, in believing I could know any-

thing to your prejudice without resenting it as much as you
should.

BALANCE

This letter, sir, which I tear in pieces to conceal the person   110
that sent it, informs me that Plume has a design upon Silvia,
and that you are privy to't.

WORTHY

Nay then, sir, I must do myself justice and endeavour to find
out the author. (*Takes up a bit*) Sir, I know the hand, and if
you refuse to discover the contents, Melinda shall tell me.   115
                                                      Going

BALANCE

Hold, sir, the contents I have told you already, only with this
circumstance, that her intimacy with Mr Worthy had drawn
the secret from him.

WORTHY

Her intimacy with me! – Dear sir, let me pick up the pieces
of this letter; 'twill give me such a hank upon her pride, to   120
have her own an intimacy under her hand; 'twas the luckiest
accident. (*Gathering up the letter*) The aspersion, sir, was
nothing but malice, the effect of a little quarrel between her
and Mrs Silvia.

BALANCE

Are you sure of that, sir?   125

WORTHY

Her maid gave me the history of part of the battle just now,
as she overheard it.

BALANCE

'Tis probable, I am satisfied.

WORTHY

But I hope, sir, your daughter has suffered nothing upon the
account?   130

BALANCE

No, no – poor girl, she's so afflicted with the news of her
brother's death that to avoid company she begged leave to
be gone into the country.

WORTHY

And is she gone?

BALANCE

I could not refuse her, she was so pressing; the coach went   135
from the door the minute before you came.

WORTHY

So pressing to be gone, sir! – I find her fortune will give her
the same airs with Melinda, and then Plume and I may

laugh at one another.

BALANCE
Like enough; women are as subject to pride as we are, and   140
why mayn't great women as well as great men forget their old
acquaintance? But come, where's this young fellow? I love
him so well it would break the heart of me to think him a
rascal. – (*Aside*) I'm glad my daughter's gone fairly off
though. – Where does the captain quarter?   145

WORTHY
At Horton's; I'm to meet him there two hours hence, and we
should be glad of your company.

BALANCE
Your pardon, dear Worthy, I must allow a day or two to the
death of my son; the decorum of mourning is what we owe
the world because they pay it to us. Afterwards, I'm yours   150
over a bottle, or how you will.

WORTHY
Sir, I'm your humble servant.   *Exeunt severally*

[Act II], Scene iii

The Street

Enter KITE, [*leading* COSTAR PEARMAIN *in one hand, and* THOMAS
APPLETREE *in the other, both drunk*]

KITE (*Sings*)
           Our prentice Tom may now refuse
           To wipe his scoundrel master's shoes,
           For now he's free to sing and play,
           Over the hills and far away.
                Over, &c.   5
              [APPLETREE *and* PEARMAIN *join in the chorus*]
           We all shall lead more happy lives,
           By getting rid of brats and wives,
           That scold and brawl both night and day,
           Over the hills and far away.
                Over, &c.   10
Hey, boys! Thus we soldiers live; drink, sing, dance, play;
we live, as one should say – we live – 'tis impossible to tell
how we live. We're all princes – why – why, you're a king –
you're an emperor, and I'm a prince – now – an't we? –

APPLETREE
No, Sergeant – I'll be no emperor.   15

KITE
> No?

APPLETREE
> No, I'll be a justice of peace.

KITE
> A justice of peace, man!

APPLETREE
> Aye, wauns will I, for since this Pressing Act they are greater
> than any emperor under the sun.   20

KITE
> Done; you're a justice of peace, and you're a king, and I'm a
> duke, and a rum duke, an't I?

PEARMAIN
> No, but I'll be no king.

KITE
> What then?

PEARMAIN
> I'll be a queen.   25

KITE
> A queen!

PEARMAIN
> Aye, Queen of England, that's greater than any king of 'em
> all.

KITE
> Bravely said, faith! Huzza for the Queen!   *All huzza*
> But hark'ee you Mr Justice and you Mr Queen, did you ever   30
> see the Queen's picture?

BOTH
> No, no, no.

KITE
> I wonder at that; I have two of 'em set in gold, and as like
> Her Majesty, God bless the mark. (*He takes two broad pieces
> out of his pocket*) See here, they're set in gold.   35
> > *Gives one to each*

APPLETREE
> The wonderful works of Nature!   *Looking at it*

PEARMAIN
> What's this written about? Here's a posy, I believe, *Ca-ro-lus*
> – what's that, Sergeant?

KITE
> Oh, *Carolus*! Why, *Carolus* is Latin for Queen Anne, that's
> all.   40

PEARMAIN
> 'Tis a fine thing to be a scollard – Sergeant, will you part

with this? I'll buy it on you, if it come within the compass of
a crawn.

KITE

A crown! Never talk of buying; 'tis the same thing among
friends, you know, I present 'em to you both; you shall give   45
me as good a thing. Put 'em up, and remember your old
friend, when I'm *over the hills and far away.*   *Singing*
                              They sing and put up the money
                    Enter PLUME *singing*

PLUME
                    Over the hills, and o're the main,
                    To Flanders, Portugal, or Spain;
                    The Queen commands, and we'll obey,   50
                    Over the hills and far away.
Come on my men of mirth, away with it, I'll make one
among ye. – Who are these hearty lads?

KITE

Off with your hats; ounds, off with your hats; this is the
captain, the captain.   55

APPLETREE

We have seen captains afore now, mun.

PEARMAIN

Aye, and lieutenant captains too; flesh, I'se keep on my nab.

APPLETREE

And I'se scarcely d'off mine for any captain in England; my
vether's a freeholder.

PLUME

Who are these jolly lads, Sergeant?   60

KITE

A couple of honest, brave fellows that are willing to serve the
Queen; I have entertained 'em just now as volunteers under
your honour's command.

PLUME

And good entertainment they shall have; volunteers are the
men I want, those are the men fit to make soldiers, captains,   65
generals.

PEARMAIN

Wauns, Tummas, what's this? Are you listed?

APPLETREE

Flesh, not I; are you, Costar?

PEARMAIN

Wauns, not I.

KITE

What, not listed! Ha, ha, ha, a very good jest, faith.   70

PEARMAIN

Come, Tummas, we'll go whome.

APPLETREE

Aye, aye, come.

KITE

Home! For shame, gentlemen, behave yourselves better
before your captain – dear Tummas, honest Costar –

PEARMAIN

No, no, we'll be gone.   *Going*   75

KITE

Nay, then I command you to stay: I place you both sentinels
in this place for two hours to watch the motion of St Mary's
clock, you, and you the motion of St Chad's; and he that dare
stir from his post till he be relieved shall have my sword in
his guts the next minute.   80

PLUME

What's the matter, Sergeant? I'm afraid you're too rough
with these gentlemen.

KITE

I'm too mild, sir, they disobey command, sir, and one of 'em
should be shot for an example to the other.

PEARMAIN

Shot, Tummas!   85

PLUME

Come, gentlemen, what's the matter?

APPLETREE

We don't know; the noble sergeant is pleased to be in a
passion, sir – but –

KITE

They disobey command, they deny their being listed.

PEARMAIN

Nay, Sergeant, we don't downright deny it neither, that we   90
dare not do for fear of being shot; but we humbly conceive
in a civil way, and begging your worship's pardon, that we
may go home.

PLUME

That's easily known; have either of you received any of the
Queen's money?   95

APPLETREE

Not a brass farthing, sir.

KITE

Sir, they have each of 'em received three and twenty shillings and sixpence, and 'tis now in their pockets.

APPLETREE

Wauns! If I have a penny in my pocket but a bent sixpence, I'll be content to be listed, and shot into the bargain.   100

PEARMAIN

And I, look'ee here, sir.

APPLETREE

Aye, here's my stock too, nothing but the Queen's picture that the sergeant gave me just now.

KITE

See there, a broad piece, three and twenty shillings and sixpence; the t'other has the fellow on't.   105

PLUME

The case is plain, gentlemen, the goods are found upon you: those pieces of gold are worth three and twenty and sixpence each.

PEARMAIN

So it seems that *Carolus* is three and twenty shillings and sixpence in Latin.   110

APPLETREE

'Tis the same thing in the Greek, for we are listed.

PEARMAIN

Flesh, but we an't, Tummas; I desire to be carried before the mayar, Captain.

While they talk, the CAPTAIN *and* SERGEANT *whisper*

PLUME

'Twill never do, Kite; your damned tricks will ruin me at last – I won't lose the fellows though, if I can help it. – Well,   115
gentlemen, there must be some trick in this; my sergeant offers to take his oath that you're fairly listed.

APPLETREE

Why, Captain, we know that you soldiers have more liberty of conscience than other folks, but for me or neighbour Costar here to take such an oath, 'twould be downright   120
perjuration.

PLUME

Look'ee you rascal, you villain, if I find that you have imposed upon these two honest fellows, I'll trample you to death, you dog; come, how was't?

APPLETREE

Nay, then we will speak. Your sergeant, as you say, is a rogue,   125
begging your worship's pardon, and –

PEARMAIN

Nay, Tummas, let me speak, you know I can read. – And so,

sir, he gave us those two pieces of money for pictures of the
Queen by way of a present.

PLUME

How! By way of a present! The son of a whore! I'll teach   130
him to abuse honest fellows like you. Scoundrel, rogue,
villain, *etc.*   *Beats off the* SERGEANT, *and follows*

BOTH

O brave, noble Captain! Huzza! A brave captain, faith.

PEARMAIN

Now, Tummas, *Carolus* is Latin for a beating; this is the
bravest captain I ever saw. – Wauns, I have a month's mind   135
to go with him.

Enter PLUME

PLUME

A dog, to abuse two such honest fellows as you! Look'ee,
gentlemen, I love a pretty fellow; I come among you here as
an officer to list soldiers, not as a kidnapper to steal slaves.

PEARMAIN

Mind that, Tummas.   140

PLUME

I desire no man to go with me, but as I went myself: I went
a volunteer, as you or you may go, for a little time carried a
musket, and now I command a company.

APPLETREE

Mind that, Costar, a sweet gentleman.

PLUME

'Tis true, gentlemen, I might take an advantage of you; the   145
Queen's money was in your pockets, my sergeant was ready
to take his oath you were listed; but I scorn to do a base thing,
you are both of you at your liberty.

PEARMAIN

Thank you, noble Captain. – I cod, I can't find in my heart
to leave him, he talks so finely.   150

APPLETREE

Aye, Costar, would he always hold in this mind?

PLUME

Come, my lads, one thing more I'll tell you: you're both
young, tight fellows, and the army is the place to make you
men forever: every man has his lot, and you have yours.
What think you now of a purse full of French gold out of a   155
monsieur's pocket, after you have dashed out his brains with
the butt of your firelock, eh?

PEARMAIN
Wauns, I'll have it, Captain – give me a shilling, I'll follow
you to the end of the world.

APPLETREE
Nay, dear Costar, duna; be advised.   160

PLUME
Here, my hero, here are two guineas for thee, as earnest of
what I'll do farther for thee.

APPLETREE
Duna take it, duna, dear Costar.
                    (*Cries, and pulls back his arm*)

PEARMAIN
I wull, I wull – wauns, my mind gives me that I shall be a
captain myself. I take your money, sir, and now I'm a   165
gentleman.

PLUME
Give me thy hand. – And now you and I will travel the world
o'er, and command wherever we tread. – [*Aside to*
PEARMAIN] Bring your friend with you if you can.

PEARMAIN
Well, Tummas, must we part?   170

APPLETREE
No, Costar, I cannot leave thee. Come, Captain (*crying*), I'll
e'en go along too, and if you have two honester, simpler lads
in your company than we twa been – I'll say no more.

PLUME
Here, my lad. (*Gives him money*) Now your name?

APPLETREE
Thummas Appletree.   175

PLUME
And yours?

PEARMAIN
Costar Pearmain.

PLUME
Born where?

APPLETREE
Both in Herefordshire.

PLUME
Very well. Courage, my lads, now we'll sing *Over the hills*   180
and far away.
            Courage, boys, 'tis one to ten,
            But we return all gentlemen;
            While conquering colours we display,

Over the hills and far away.　　　　　　　　185
Over, &c.　　　　　　　　　　　　*Exeunt*

Act III, Scene i

The Market-place
Enter PLUME *and* WORTHY

WORTHY
I can't forbear admiring the equality of our two fortunes: we
loved two ladies, they met us halfway, and just as we were
upon the point of leaping into their arms, fortune drops into
their laps, pride possesses their hearts, a maggot fills their
heads, madness takes 'em by the tails, they snort, kick up their　5
heels, and away they run.

PLUME
And leave us here to mourn upon the shore – a couple of
poor, melancholy monsters – what shall we do?

WORTHY
I have a trick for mine; the letter, you know, and the fortune-
teller.　　　　　　　　　　　　　　　　　　　　　　10

PLUME
And I have a trick for mine.

WORTHY
What is't?

PLUME
I'll never think of her again.

WORTHY
No!

PLUME
No; I think myself above administering to the pride of any　15
woman, were she worth twelve thousand a year, and I han't
the vanity to believe I shall ever gain a lady worth twelve
hundred; the generous, good-natured Silvia in her smock I
admire, but the haughty, scornful Silvia, with her fortune,
I despise.　　　　　　　　　　　　　　　　　　　　20

A SONG

1

Come, fair one, be kind,
You never shall find
A fellow so fit for a lover;
The world shall view

My passion for you,   25
But never your passion discover.

2

I still will complain
Of your frowns and disdain,
Though I revel through all your charms;
The world shall declare,   30
That I die with despair,
When I only die in your arms.

3

I still will adore,
And love more and more,
But, by Jove, if you chance to prove cruel: 35
I'll get me a miss
That freely will kiss,
Though I afterwards drink water-gruel.

What, sneak out o'town and not so much as a word, a line, a
compliment – 'sdeath! How far off does she live? I'll go and   40
break her windows.

KITE
Ha, ha, ha; aye, and the window bars too to come at her.
Come, come, friend, no more of your rough, military airs.

Enter KITE

KITE
Captain, sir, look yonder, she's a-coming this way, 'tis the
prettiest, cleanest, little tit.   45

PLUME
Now, Worthy, to show you how much I'm in love – here she
comes, and what is that great country fellow with her?

KITE
I can't tell, sir.

Enter ROSE *and her brother* BULLOCK, ROSE *with a basket on her
arm, crying 'Chickens'*

ROSE
Buy chickens, young and tender, young and tender chickens.

PLUME
Here, you chickens!   50

ROSE
Who calls?

PLUME
Come hither, pretty maid.
ROSE
Will you please to buy, sir?
WORTHY
Yes, child, we'll both buy.
PLUME
Nay, Worthy, that's not fair, market for yourself; come,   55
child, I'll buy all you have.
ROSE
Then all I have is at your sarvice.   *Curtsies*
WORTHY
Then I must shift for myself, I find.   *Exit*
PLUME
Let me see – young and tender, you say?

Chucks her under the chin
ROSE
As ever you tasted in your life, sir.   *Curtsies*   60
PLUME
Come, I must examine your basket to the bottom, my dear.
ROSE
Nay, for that matter, put in your hand; feel, sir; I warrant
my ware as good as any in the market.
PLUME
And I'll buy it all, child, were it ten times more.
ROSE
Sir, I can furnish you.   65
PLUME
Come then; we won't quarrel about the price, they're fine
birds; pray what's your name, pretty creature?
ROSE
Rose, sir; my father is a farmer within three short mile o'th'
town; we keep this market; I sell chickens, eggs, and butter,
and my brother Bullock there sells corn.   70
BULLOCK
Come, sister, haste ye; we shall be liate a whome.

All this while BULLOCK *whistles about the stage*
PLUME
Kite! (*Tips him the wink, he returns it*) Pretty Mrs Rose – you
have – let me see – how many?
ROSE
A dozen, sir, and they are richly worth a crawn.

BULLOCK

Come, Ruose, Ruose, I sold fifty stracke o'barley today in   75
half this time; but you will higgle and higgle for a penny
more than the commodity is worth.

ROSE

What's that to you, oaf? I can make as much out of a groat
as you can out of fourpence, I'm sure – the gentleman bids
fair, and when I meet with a chapman, I know how to make   80
the best on him – and so, sir, I say for a crawn piece the
bargain's yours.

PLUME

Here's a guinea, my dear.

ROSE

I con't change your money, sir.

PLUME

Indeed, indeed but you can – my lodging is hard by, chicken,   85
and we'll make change there.   *Goes off, she follows him*

KITE

So, sir, as I was telling you, I have seen one of these hussars
eat up a ravelin for his breakfast and afterwards pick his teeth
with a palisado.

BULLOCK

Aye, you soldiers see very strange things – but pray, sir,   90
what is a ravelin?

KITE

Why 'tis like a modern minced pie, but the crust is confounded hard, and the plums are somewhat hard of
digestion!

BULLOCK

Then your palisado, pray what may he be? – Come, Ruose,   95
pray ha' done.

KITE

Your palisado is a pretty sort of bodkin about the thickness
of my leg.

BULLOCK

(*Aside*) – That's a fib, I believe. – Eh, where's Ruose?
Ruose! Ruose! 'sflesh, where's Ruose gone?   100

KITE

She's gone with the captain.

BULLOCK

The captain! Wauns, there's no pressing of women, sure?

KITE

But there is, sir.

BULLOCK

If the captain should press Ruose, I should be ruined;
which way went she? – Oh, the devil take your rablins and   105
palisaders.   *Exit*

KITE

You shall be better acquainted with them, honest Bullock, or
I shall miss of my aim.

Enter WORTHY

WORTHY

Why, thou'rt the most useful fellow in nature to your
captain, admirable in your way, I find.   110

KITE

Yes, sir, I understand my business, I will say it; you must
know, sir, I was born a gypsy, and bred among that crew till
I was ten year old, there I learned canting and lying; I was
bought from my mother Cleopatra by a certain nobleman
for three pistoles, who liking my beauty made me his page,   115
there I learned impudence and pimping; I was turned off for
wearing my lord's linen, and drinking my lady's ratafia; and
then turned bailiff's follower, there I learned bullying and
swearing. I at last got into the army, and there I learned
whoring and drinking. – So that if your worship pleases to   120
cast up the whole sum, viz., canting, lying, impudence,
pimping, bullying, swearing, whoring, drinking, and a
halberd, you will find the sum total will amount to a
recruiting sergeant.

WORTHY

And pray, what induced you to turn soldier?   125

KITE

Hunger and ambition – the fears of starving and hopes of a
truncheon led me along to a gentleman with a fair tongue
and fair periwig, who loaded me with promises; but I gad
'twas the lightest load that I ever felt in my life – he
promised to advance me, and indeed he did so – to a garret   130
in the Savoy. I asked him why he put me in prison; he called
me lying dog, and said I was in garrison; and indeed 'tis a
garrison that may hold out till doomsday before I should
desire to take it again. But here comes Justice Balance.

Enter BALANCE *and* BULLOCK

BALANCE

Here, you Sergeant, where's your captain? Here's a poor,   135
foolish fellow comes clamouring to me with a complaint, that

your captain has pressed his sister; do you know anything of
this matter, Worthy?

WORTHY

Ha, ha, ha, I know his sister is gone with Plume to his
lodgings to sell him some chickens.   140

BALANCE

Is that all? The fellow's a fool.

BULLOCK

I know that, an't please you; but if your worship pleases to
grant me a warrant to bring her before you for fear o' th'
worst.

BALANCE

Thou'rt mad, fellow, thy sister's safe enough.   145

KITE (*Aside*)

I hope so too.

WORTHY

Hast thou no more sense, fellow, than to believe that the
captain can list women?

BULLOCK

I know not whether they list them, or what they do with
them, but I'm sure they carry as many women as men with   150
them out of the country.

BALANCE

But how came you not to go along with your sister?

BULLOCK

Luord, sir, I thought no more of her going than I do of the
day I shall die; but this gentleman here, not suspecting any
hurt neither, I believe – you thought no harm, friend, did ye?   155

KITE

Lack-a-day, sir, not I. – (*Aside*) Only that I believe I shall
marry her tomorrow.

BALANCE

I begin to smell powder. Well, friend, but what did that
gentleman with you?

BULLOCK

'Why, sir, he entertained me with a fine story of a great fight   160
between the Hungarians, I think it was, and the Irish.

KITE

And so, sir, while we were in the heat of the battle, the
captain carried off the baggage.

BALANCE

Sergeant, go along with this fellow to your captain, give him
my humble service, and desire him to discharge the wench,   165
though he has listed her.

BULLOCK
　Aye – and if he ben't free for that, he shall have another man
　in her place.

KITE
　Come, honest friend. – (*Aside*) You shall go to my quarters
　instead of the captain's.　　　　*Exeunt* KITE *and* BULLOCK　170

BALANCE
　We must get this mad captain his complement of men, and
　send him a-packing, else he'll overrun the country.

WORTHY
　You see, sir, how little he values your daughter's disdain.

BALANCE
　I like him the better; I was much such another fellow at his
　age; I never set my heart upon any woman so much as to　175
　make me uneasy at the disappointment; but what was very
　surprising both to myself and friends, I changed o' th' sudden
　from the most fickle lover to the most constant husband in the
　world. But how goes your affair with Melinda?

WORTHY
　Very slowly. Cupid had formerly wings, but I think in this　180
　age he goes upon crutches, or I fancy Venus had been
　dallying with her cripple Vulcan when my amour com-
　menced, which has made it go on so lamely. My mistress has
　got a captain too, but such a captain! As I live, yonder he
　comes.　　　　185

BALANCE
　Who? That bluff fellow in the sash? I don't know him.

WORTHY
　But I engage he knows you, and everybody at first sight; his
　impudence were a prodigy, were not his ignorance pro-
　portionable; he has the most universal acquaintance of any
　man living, for he won't be alone, and nobody will keep him　190
　company twice; then he's a Caesar among the women, *veni*,
　vidi, *vici*, that's all. If he has but talked with the maid, he
　swears he has lain with the mistress; but the most surprising
　part of his character is his memory, which is the most
　prodigious, and the most trifling in the world.　　　　195

BALANCE
　I have met with such men, and I take this good-for-nothing
　memory to proceed from a certain contexture of the brain,
　which is purely adapted to impertinencies, and there they
　lodge secure, the owner having no thoughts of his own to
　disturb them. I have known a man as perfect as a chronologer　200
　as to the day and year of most important transactions, but be

altogether ignorant of the causes, springs, or consequences
of any one thing of moment; I have known another acquire
so much by travel, as to tell you the names of most places in
Europe, with their distances of miles, leagues, or hours, as   205
punctually as a post-boy; but for anything else, as ignorant
as the horse that carries the mail.

WORTHY
This is your man, sir, add but the traveller's privilege of
lying, and even that he abuses; this is the picture, behold the
life.   210

Enter BRAZEN

BRAZEN
Mr Worthy, I'm your servant, and so forth – hark'ee, my
dear –

WORTHY
Whispering, sir, before company is not manners, and when
nobody's by, 'tis foolish.

BRAZEN
Company! *Mort de ma vie,* I beg the gentleman's pardon,   215
who is he?

WORTHY
Ask him.

BRAZEN
So I will. – My dear, I'm your servant, and so forth, – your
name, my dear?

BALANCE
Very laconic, sir.   220

BRAZEN
Laconic, a very good name truly; I have known several of
the Laconics abroad. Poor Jack Laconic! He was killed at
the battle of Landen. I remember that he had a blue ribband
in his hat that very day, and after he fell, we found a piece of
neat's tongue in his pocket.   225

BALANCE
Pray, sir, did the French attack us or we them at Landen?

BRAZEN
The French attack us! Oons, sir, are you a Jacobite?

BALANCE
Why that question?

BRAZEN
Because none but a Jacobite could think that the French
durst attack us – no, sir, we attacked them on the – I have   230
reason to remember the time, for I had two-and-twenty

horses killed under me that day.

BALANCE

Or perhaps, sir, like my countryman, you rid upon half a
dozen horses at once.   235

BRAZEN

What d'e mean, gentlemen? I tell you they were killed, all
torn to pieces by cannon-shot, except six that I staked to
death upon the enemy's *chevaux de frise.*

BALANCE

Noble Captain, may I crave your name?

BRAZEN

Brazen, at your service.   240

BALANCE

Oh, Brazen, a very good name, I have known several of the
Brazens abroad.

WORTHY

Do you know Captain Plume, sir?

BRAZEN

Is he anything related to Frank Plume in Northamptonshire?
– Honest Frank! Many, many a dry bottle have we cracked   245
hand to fist; you must have known his brother Charles that
was concerned in the India Company, he married the
daughter of old Tongue-Pad, the Master in Chancery, a very
pretty woman, only squinted a little; she died in childbed of
her first child, but the child survived, 'twas a daughter, but 250
whether 'twas called Margaret or Marjory, upon my soul I
can't remember – but, gentlemen (*looking on his watch*), I
must meet a lady, a twenty-thousand-pounder, presently,
upon the walk by the water – Worthy, your servant; Laconic,
yours.   *Exit*   255

BALANCE

If you can have so mean an opinion of Melinda, as to be
jealous of this fellow, I think she ought to give you cause to
be so.

WORTHY

I don't think she encourages him so much for gaining herself
a lover, as to set me up a rival; were there any credit to be 260
given to his words, I should believe Melinda had made him
this assignation; I must go see – sir, you'll pardon me.

BALANCE

Aye, aye, sir, you're a man of business.   [*Exit* WORTHY]
But what have we got here?

Enter ROSE *singing*

ROSE

And I shall be a lady, a captain's lady, and ride single upon   265
a white horse with a star, upon a velvet sidesaddle; and I
shall go to London and see the tombs and the lions, and the
Queen. Sir, an't please your worship, I have often seen your
worship ride through our grounds a-hunting, begging your
worship's pardon – pray, what may this lace be worth a yard?   270
                                            Showing some lace

BALANCE

Right Mechlin, by this light! Where did you get this lace,
child?

ROSE

No matter for that, sir, I come honestly by't.

BALANCE

I question it much.

ROSE

And see here, sir, a fine turkey-shell snuff-box, and fine   275
mangeree, see here: (*takes snuff affectedly*) the captain learnt
me how to take it with an air.

BALANCE

Oho, the captain! Now the murder's out – and so the
captain taught you to take it with an air?

ROSE

Yes, and give it with an air too – will your worship please to   280
taste my snuff?   *Offers the box affectedly*

BALANCE

You're a very apt scholar, pretty maid. And pray what did
you give the captain for these fine things?

ROSE

He's to have my brother for a soldier, and two or three sweet-
hearts that I have in the country, they shall all go with the   285
captain. Oh, he's the finest man, and the humblest withal;
would you believe it, sir, he carried me up with him to his
own chamber with as much familiarity as if I had been the
best lady in the land.

BALANCE

Oh, he's a mighty familiar gentleman as can be.   290

Enter PLUME *singing*

PLUME

    But it is not so
    With those that go

> Through frost and snow
> Most apropos,
> My maid with the milking-pail.   295
> > *Takes hold on* ROSE

How, the justice! Then I'm arraigned, condemned, and
executed.

BALANCE
Oh, my noble Captain.

ROSE
And my noble captain too, sir.

PLUME
'Sdeath, child, are you mad? – Mr Balance, I am so full of   300
business about my recruits, that I han't a moment's time to –
I have just now three or four people to –

BALANCE
Nay, Captain, I must speak to you.

ROSE
And so must I too, Captain.

PLUME
Any other time, sir – I cannot for my life, sir –   305

BALANCE
Pray, sir.

PLUME
Twenty thousand things – I would but – now, sir, pray –
devil take me – I cannot – I must –   *Breaks away*

BALANCE
Nay, I'll follow you.   *Exit*

ROSE
And I too.   *Exit*   310

[Act III], Scene ii

The Walk by the Severn side
Enter MELINDA *and her maid* LUCY

MELINDA
And pray, was it a ring, or buckle, or pendants, or knots; or
in what shape was the almighty gold transformed that has
bribed you so much in his favour?

LUCY
Indeed, madam, the last bribe I had was from the captain,
and that was only a small piece of Flanders edging for   5
pinners.

MELINDA
Aye, Flanders lace is as constant a present from officers to
their women as something else is from their women to them.
They every year bring over a cargo of lace to cheat the
Queen of her duty, and her subjects of their honesty.   10

LUCY
They only barter one sort of prohibited goods for another,
madam.

MELINDA
Has any of them been bartering with you, Mrs Pert, that you
talk so like a trader?

LUCY
Madam, you talk as peevishly to me as if it were my fault,   15
the crime is none of mine though I pretend to excuse it;
though he should not see you this week, can I help it? But as
I was saying, madam, his friend Captain Plume has so taken
him up these two days –

MELINDA
Psha! Would his friend, the captain, were tied upon his back;   20
I warrant he has never been sober since that confounded
captain came to town; the devil take all officers, I say – they
do the nation more harm by debauching us at home, than
they do good by defending us abroad: no sooner a captain
comes to town, but all the young fellows flock about him,   25
and we can't keep a man to ourselves.

LUCY
One would imagine, madam, by your concern for Worthy's
absence, that you should use him better when he's with you.

MELINDA
Who told you, pray, that I was concerned for his absence?
I'm only vexed that I've had nothing said to me these two   30
days: one may like the love and despise the lover, I hope; as
one may love the treason and hate the traitor. Oh! Here
comes another captain, and a rogue that has the confidence
to make love to me; but indeed I don't wonder at that, when
he has the assurance to fancy himself a fine gentleman.   35

LUCY (*Aside*)
If he should speak o' th' assignation, I should be ruined.

Enter BRAZEN

BRAZEN
True to the touch, faith. (*Aside*) I'll draw up all my com-
pliments into one grand platoon, and fire upon her at once.

Thou peerless princess of Salopian plains,
Envied by nymphs and worshipped by the swains,   40
Behold how humbly does the Severn glide,
To greet thee, princess of the Severn side.
Madam, I'm your humble servant and all that, madam – a
fine river this same Severn – do you love fishing, madam?

MELINDA

'Tis a pretty melancholy amusement for lovers.   45

BRAZEN

I'll go buy hooks and lines presently; for you must know,
madam, that I have served in Flanders against the French,
in Hungary against the Turks, and in Tangier against the
Moors, and I was never so much in love before; and split me,
madam, in all the campaigns I ever made I have not seen so   50
fine a woman as your ladyship.

MELINDA

And from all the men I ever saw I never had so fine a
compliment; but you soldiers are the best-bred men, that
we must allow.

BRAZEN

Some of us, madam, but there are brutes among us too, very   55
sad brutes; for my own part, I have always had the good luck
to prove agreeable – I have had very considerable offers,
madam, I might have married a German princess worth fifty
thousand crowns a year, but her stove disgusted me. – The
daughter of a Turkish bashaw fell in love with me too when   60
I was prisoner among the infidels; she offered to rob her
father of his treasure, and make her escape with me, but I
don't know how, my time was not come; hanging and
marriage, you know, go by destiny; Fate has reserved me
for a Shropshire lady with twenty thousand pound – do   65
you know any such person, madam?

MELINDA

Extravagant coxcomb! – To be sure, a great many ladies of
that fortune would be proud of the name of Mrs Brazen.

BRAZEN

Nay, for that matter, madam, there are women of very good
quality of the name of Brazen.   70

Enter WORTHY

MELINDA

Oh, are you there, gentleman? – Come, Captain, we'll walk
this way, give me your hand.

BRAZEN
My hand, heart's blood, and guts are at your service. –
Mr Worthy – your servant, my dear. *Exit leading* MELINDA
WORTHY
Death and fire! This is not to be borne.   75

Enter PLUME

PLUME
No more it is, faith.
WORTHY
What?
PLUME
The March beer at the Raven; I have been doubly serving
the Queen, – raising men and raising the excise – recruiting
and elections are rare friends to the excise.   80
WORTHY
You an't drunk?
PLUME
No, no, whimsical only; I could be mighty foolish, and
fancy myself mighty witty; Reason still keeps its throne,
but it nods a little, that's all.
WORTHY
Then you're just fit for a frolic?   85
PLUME
As fit as close pinners for a punk in the pit.
WORTHY
There's your play then, recover me that vessel from that
Tangerine.
PLUME
She's well rigged, but how is she manned?
WORTHY
By Captain Brazen that I told you of today; she is called 90
the Melinda, a first rate I can assure you; she sheered off
with him just now on purpose to affront me, but according
to your advice I would take no notice, because I would
seem to be above a concern for her behaviour. But have a
care of a quarrel.   95
PLUME
No, no, I never quarrel with anything in my cups but an
oyster wench or a cook maid, and if they ben't civil, I knock
'em down. But hark'ee my friend, I will make love, and I
must make love. I tell'ee what, I'll make love like a platoon.
WORTHY
Platoon, how's that?   100

PLUME

  I'll kneel, stoop, and stand, faith; most ladies are gained by
platooning.

WORTHY

  Here they come; I must leave you.   *Exit*

PLUME

  So – now must I look as sober and demure as a whore at a
christening.   105

Enter BRAZEN *and* MELINDA

BRAZEN

  Who's that, madam?

MELINDA

  A brother officer of yours, I suppose, sir.

BRAZEN

  Aye! – (*To* PLUME) My dear.

PLUME

  My dear!   *They run and embrace*

BRAZEN

  My dear boy, how is't? – Your name, my dear? If I be not   110
mistaken, I have seen your face.

PLUME

  I never see yours in my life, my dear – but there's a face
well known as the sun's, that shines on all and is by all
adored.

BRAZEN

  Have you any pretensions, sir?   115

PLUME

  Pretensions!

BRAZEN

  That is, sir, have you ever served abroad?

PLUME

  I have served at home, sir, for ages served this cruel fair –
and that will serve the turn, sir.

MELINDA (*Aside*)

  So, between the fool and the rake I shall bring a fine spot of   120
work upon my hands – I see Worthy yonder, I could be
content to be friends with him would he come this way.

BRAZEN

  Will you fight for the lady, sir?

PLUME

  No, sir, but I'll have her notwithstanding.

    Thou peerless princess of Salopian plains,   125
    Envied by nymphs and worshipped by the swains—

BRAZEN
Oons, sir, not fight for her!

PLUME
Prithee be quiet, I shall be out –
Behold how humbly does the Severn glide
To greet thee, princess of the Severn side.   130

BRAZEN
Don't mind him, madam. – If he were not so well dressed I
should take him for a poet; but I'll show the difference
presently – come, madam, we'll place you between us, and
now the longest sword carries her.

Draws, MELINDA *shrieks*

Enter WORTHY

MELINDA
Oh, Mr Worthy, save me from these madmen.   135

Runs off with WORTHY

PLUME
Ha, ha, ha, why don't you follow, sir, and fight the bold
ravisher?

BRAZEN
No, sir, you're my man.

PLUME
I don't like the wages, and I won't be your man.

BRAZEN
Then you're not worth my sword.   140

PLUME
No? Pray what did it cost?

BRAZEN
It cost me twenty pistoles in France, and my enemies
thousands of lives in Flanders.

PLUME
Then they had a dear bargain.

Enter SILVIA *dressed in man's apparel*

SILVIA
Save ye, save ye, gentlemen.   145

BRAZEN
My dear, I'm yours.

PLUME
Do you know the gentleman?

BRAZEN
No, but I will presently. – Your name, my dear?

SILVIA
Wilful, Jack Wilful, at your service.
BRAZEN
What! The Kentish Wilfuls or those of Staffordshire?   150
SILVIA
Both, sir, both; I'm related to all the Wilfuls in Europe,
and I'm head of the family at present.
PLUME
Do you live in this country, sir?
SILVIA
Yes, sir, I live where I stand, I have neither home, house,
nor habitation beyond this spot of ground.   155
BRAZEN
What are you, sir?
SILVIA
A rake.
PLUME
In the army, I presume.
SILVIA
No, but intend to list immediately – look'ee, gentlemen,
he that bids me fairest has me.   160
BRAZEN
Sir, I'll prefer you, I'll make you a corporal this minute.
PLUME
A corporal! I'll make you my companion, you shall eat with
me.
BRAZEN
You shall drink with me.
PLUME
You shall lie with me, you young rogue.   *Kisses her*   165
BRAZEN
You shall receive your pay and do no duty.
SILVIA
Then you must make me a field-officer.
PLUME
Pho, pho, I'll do more than all this, I'll make you a corporal,
and give you a brevet for sergeant.
BRAZEN
Can you read and write, sir?   170
SILVIA
Yes.
BRAZEN
Then your business is done, I'll make you chaplain to the
regiment.

SILVIA
Your promises are so equal that I'm at a loss to choose;
there is one Plume that I hear much commended in town,   175
pray which of you is Captain Plume?

PLUME
I am Captain Plume.

BRAZEN
No, no, I'm Captain Plume.

SILVIA
Hey day!

PLUME
Captain Plume, I'm your servant, my dear.   180

BRAZEN
Captain Brazen, I'm yours. – The fellow dare not fight.

Enter KITE

KITE
Sir, if you please –   *Goes to whisper* PLUME

PLUME
No, no, there's your captain. – Captain Plume, your sergeant here has got so drunk he mistakes me for you.

BRAZEN
He's an incorrigible sot. – Here, my Hector of Holborn, 185
forty shillings for you.

PLUME
I forbid the banns – look'ee, friend, you shall list with
Captain Brazen.

SILVIA
I will see Captain Brazen hanged first, I will list with
Captain Plume; I'm a freeborn Englishman and will be a 190
slave my own way. – (*To* BRAZEN) Look'ee, sir, will you stand
by me?

BRAZEN
I warrant you, my lad.

SILVIA
Then I will tell you, Captain Brazen (*to* PLUME), that you
are an ignorant, pretending, impudent coxcomb.   195

BRAZEN
Aye, aye, a sad dog.

SILVIA
A very sad dog; give me the money, noble Captain Plume.

PLUME
Then you won't list with Captain Brazen?

SILVIA

I won't.

BRAZEN

Never mind him, child, I'll end the dispute presently; 200
hark'ee, my dear –

Takes PLUME *to one side of the stage and entertains him in
dumb show*

KITE

Sir, he in the plain coat is Captain Plume; I'm his sergeant
and will take my oath on't.

SILVIA

What! You are Sergeant Kite?

KITE

At your service.   205

SILVIA

Then I would not take your oath for a farthing.

KITE

A very understanding youth of his age. Pray, sir, let me
look you full in the face.

SILVIA

Well, sir, what have you to say to my face?

KITE

The very image and superscription of my brother, two   210
bullets of the same calibre were never so like; sure it must
be Charles, Charles –

SILVIA

What d'ye mean by Charles?

KITE

The voice too, only a little variation in effa ut flat; my dear
brother, for I must call you so, if you should have the   215
fortune to enter into the most noble society of the sword, I
bespeak you for a comrade.

SILVIA

No, sir, I'll be your captain's comrade if anybody's.

KITE

Ambition! There again, 'tis a noble passion for a soldier; by
that I gained this glorious halberd. Ambition! I see a com-   220
mission in his face already; pray, noble Captain, give me
leave to salute you.   *Offers to kiss her*

SILVIA

What, men kiss one another!

KITE

We officers do, 'tis our way; we live together like man and

wife, always either kissing or fighting. – But I see a storm   225
a-coming.

SILVIA

Now, Sergeant, I shall see who is your captain by your
knocking down the t'other.

KITE

My captain scorns assistance, sir.

BRAZEN

How dare you contend for anything and not dare to draw   230
your sword? But you're a young fellow, and have not been
much abroad, I excuse that; but prithee resign the man,
prithee do; you're a very honest fellow.

PLUME

You lie, and you're a son of a whore.

Draws, and makes up to BRAZEN

BRAZEN (*Retiring*)

Hold, hold, did not you refuse to fight for the lady?   235

PLUME

I always do – but for a man I'll fight knee deep, so you lie
again.

PLUME *and* BRAZEN *fight a traverse or two about the stage;*
SILVIA *draws, and is held by* KITE, *who sounds to arms with his*
mouth, takes SILVIA *in his arms, and carries her off the stage*

BRAZEN

Hold – where's the man?

PLUME

Gone.

BRAZEN

Then what do we fight for? (*Puts up*) Now let's embrace,   240
my dear.

PLUME

With all my heart, my dear. (*Putting up*) I suppose Kite
has listed him by this time.   *They embrace*

BRAZEN

You're a brave fellow. I always fight with a man before I
make him my friend; and if once I find he will fight, I never   245
quarrel with him afterwards. – And now I'll tell you a
secret, my dear friend, that lady we frighted out o'the walk
just now I found in bed this morning, so beautiful, so
inviting – I presently locked the door – but I'm a man of
honour – but I believe I shall marry her nevertheless; her   250
twenty thousand pound, you know, will be a pretty con-
veniency – I had an assignation with her here, but your

coming spoiled my sport, curse ye, my dear, – but don't do
so again.

PLUME

No, no, my dear, men are my business at present.   255

Exeunt

Act IV, Scene i

The Walk by the Severn side
[Enter] ROSE *and* BULLOCK *meeting*

ROSE

Where have you been, you great booby? You're always out
o' th'way in the time of preferment.

BULLOCK

Preferment! Who should prefer me?

ROSE

I would prefer you; who should prefer a man but a woman?
Come throw away that great club, hold up your head,   5
cock your hat, and look big.

BULLOCK

Ah! Ruose, Ruose, I fear somebody will look big sooner
than folk think of; this genteel breeding never comes into
the country without a train of followers. – Here has been
Cartwheel your sweetheart, what will become o' him?   10

ROSE

Look'ee, I'm a great woman and will provide for my rela-
tions; I told the captain how finely he played upon the
tabor and pipe, so he has set him down for drum-major.

BULLOCK

Nay, sister, why did not you keep that place for me? You
know I always loved to be a-drumming, if it were but on a   15
table, or on a quart pot.

Enter SILVIA

SILVIA

Had I but a commission in my pocket I fancy my breeches
would become me as well as any ranting fellow of 'em all;
for I take a bold step, a rakish toss, a smart cock, and an
impudent air to be the principal ingredients in the com-   20
position of a captain. – What's here? Rose, my nurse's
daughter. I'll go and practise. – Come, child, kiss me at
once. (*Kisses* ROSE) And her brother too. – Well, honest
Dungfork, do you know the difference between a horse cart
and a cart horse, eh?   25

BULLOCK

I presume that your worship is a captain by your clothes
and your courage.

SILVIA

Suppose I were, would you be contented to list, friend?

ROSE

No, no, though your worship be a handsome man, there be
others as fine as you; my brother is engaged to Captain   30
Plume.

SILVIA

Plume! Do you know Captain Plume?

ROSE

Yes, I do, and he knows me. – He took the very ribbands
out of his shirtsleeves and put 'em into my shoes – see
there. – I can assure you that I can do anything with the   35
captain.

BULLOCK

That is, in a modest way, sir. – Have a care what you say,
Ruose, don't shame your parentage.

ROSE

Nay, for that matter I am not so simple as to say that I can
do anything with the captain, but what I may do with any-   40
body else.

SILVIA

So! And pray what do you expect from this captain, child?

ROSE

I expect, sir! I expect – but he ordered me to tell nobody –
but suppose that he should promise to marry me?

SILVIA

You should have a care, my dear, men will promise any-   45
thing beforehand.

ROSE

I know that, but he promised to marry me afterwards.

BULLOCK

Wauns, Ruose, what have you said?

SILVIA

Afterwards! After what?

ROSE

After I had sold him my chickens. – I hope there's no   50
harm in that.

Enter PLUME

PLUME

What, Mr Wilful, so close with my market-woman!

SILVIA

(*Aside*) I'll try if he loves her. – Close, sir! aye, and closer
yet, sir. – Come, my pretty maid, you and I will withdraw a
little.   55

PLUME

No, no, friend, I han't done with her yet.

SILVIA

Nor have I begun with her, so I have as good a right as you
have.

PLUME

Thou art a bloody impudent fellow.

SILVIA

Sir, I would qualify myself for the service.   60

PLUME

Hast thou really a mind to the service?

SILVIA

Yes, sir; so let her go.

ROSE

Pray, gentlemen, don't be so violent.

PLUME

Come, leave it to the girl's own choice. – Will you belong to
me or to that gentleman?   65

ROSE

Let me consider, you're both very handsome.

PLUME

Now the natural inconstancy of her sex begins to work.

ROSE

Pray, sir, what will you give me?

BULLOCK

Dunna be angry, sir, that my sister should be mercenary,
for she's but young.   70

SILVIA

Give thee, child! – I'll set thee above scandal; you shall have
a coach with six before and six behind, an equipage to make
vice fashionable, and put virtue out of countenance.

PLUME

Pho, that's easily done, – I'll do more for thee, child, I'll
buy you a furbelow scarf, and give you a ticket to see a play.   75

BULLOCK

A play! Wauns, Ruose, take the ticket, and let's see the
show.

SILVIA

Look'ee, Captain, if you won't resign, I'll go list with
Captain Brazen this minute.

PLUME
> Will you list with me if I give up my title?   80

SILVIA
> I will.

PLUME
> Take her: I'll change a woman for a man at any time.

ROSE
> I have heard before, indeed, that you captains used to sell your men.

BULLOCK
> (*Crying*) Pray, Captain, don't send Ruose to the West   85
> Indies.

PLUME
> Ha, ha, ha, West Indies! No, no, my honest lad, give me thy hand; nor you nor she shall move a step farther than I do. – This gentleman is one of us, and will be kind to you, Mrs Rose.   90

ROSE
> But will you be so kind to me, sir, as the captain would?

SILVIA
> I can't be altogether so kind to you, my circumstances are not so good as the captain's; but I'll take care of you, upon my word.

PLUME
> Aye, aye, we'll all take care of her; she shall live like a   95
> princess, and her brother here shall be – what would you be?

BULLOCK
> Ah! sir, if you had not promised the place of drum-major –

PLUME
> Aye, that is promised – but what think ye of barrack-master? You're a person of understanding, and barrack-master you shall be. – But what's become of this same   100
> Cartwheel you told me of, my dear?

ROSE
> We'll go fetch him – come, brother barrack-master. – We shall find you at home, noble Captain?

>   *Exeunt* ROSE *and* BULLOCK

PLUME
> Yes, yes – and now, sir, here are your forty shillings.

SILVIA
> Captain Plume, I despise your listing-money; if I do serve,   105
> 'tis purely for love – of that wench I mean. For you must know, that among my other sallies, I have spent the best part of my fortune in search of a maid, and could never

find one hitherto; so you may be assured I'd not sell my
freedom under a less purchase than I did my estate. – So   110
before I list I must be certified that this girl is a virgin.

PLUME

Mr Wilful, I can't tell how you can be certified in that point,
till you try, but upon my honour she may be a vestal for
aught that I know to the contrary. – I gained her heart
indeed by some trifling presents and promises, and knowing   115
that the best security for a woman's soul is her body, I
would have made myself master of that too, had not the
jealousy of my impertinent landlady interposed.

SILVIA

So you only want an opportunity for accomplishing your
designs upon her?   120

PLUME

Not at all, I have already gained my ends, which were only
the drawing in one or two of her followers. The women, you
know, are the loadstones everywhere: gain the wives and
you're caressed by the husbands; please the mistresses and
you are valued by their gallants; secure an interest with the 125
finest women at court and you procure the favour of the
greatest men; so, kiss the prettiest country wenches and
you are sure of listing the lustiest fellows. Some people
may call this artifice, but I term it stratagem, since it is so
main a part of the service – besides, the fatigue of recruiting 130
is so intolerable, that unless we could make ourselves some
pleasure amidst the pain, no mortal man would be able to
bear it.

SILVIA

Well, sir, I'm satisfied as to the point in debate; but now let
me beg you to lay aside your recruiting airs, put on the man   135
of honour, and tell me plainly what usage I must expect when
I'm under your command.

PLUME

You must know in the first place, then, that I hate to have
gentlemen in my company, for they are always troublesome and expensive, sometimes dangerous; and 'tis a con-   140
stant maxim amongst us, that those who know the least
obey the best. Notwithstanding all this, I find something
so agreeable about you, that engages me to court your company; and I can't tell how it is, but I should be uneasy to
see you under the command of anybody else. – Your usage   145
will chiefly depend upon your behaviour; only this you
must expect, that if you commit a small fault I will excuse it,

if a great one, I'll discharge you; for something tells me I
shall not be able to punish you.

SILVIA

And something tells me, that if you do discharge me 'twill be   150
the greatest punishment you can inflict; for were we this
moment to go upon the greatest dangers in your profession,
they would be less terrible to me than to stay behind you. –
And now your hand, – this lists me – and now you are my
captain.   155

PLUME

Your friend. (*Kisses her*) 'Sdeath! There's something in this
fellow that charms me.

SILVIA

One favour I must beg – this affair will make some noise, and
I have some friends that would censure my conduct if I
threw myself into the circumstance of a private sentinel of   160
my own head; I must therefore take care to be impressed by
the Act of Parliament; you shall leave that to me.

PLUME

What you please as to that. – Will you lodge at my quarters
in the meantime? You shall have part of my bed.

SILVIA

Oh, fie, lie with a common soldier! – Would not you rather   165
lie with a common woman?

PLUME

No, faith, I'm not that rake that the world imagines; I have
got an air of freedom which people mistake for lewdness in
me, as they mistake formality in others for religion; the
world is all a cheat, only I take mine which is undesigned to   170
be more excusable than theirs, which is hypocritical; I hurt
nobody but myself, and they abuse all mankind. – Will you
lie with me?

SILVIA

No, no, Captain, you forget Rose, she's to be my bedfellow
you know.   175

PLUME

I had forgot, pray be kind to her.   *Exeunt severally*

Enter MELINDA *and* LUCY

MELINDA

'Tis the greatest misfortune in nature for a woman to want a
confidante: we are so weak that we can do nothing without
assistance, and then a secret racks us worse than the colic;
I'm at this minute so sick of a secret that I'm ready to faint   180

away – help me, Lucy.

LUCY

Bless me, madam, what's the matter?

MELINDA

Vapours only – I begin to recover – if Silvia were in town, I could heartily forgive her faults for the ease of discovering my own.   185

LUCY

You're thoughtful, madam; am not I worthy to know the cause?

MELINDA

You're a servant, and a secret would make you saucy.

LUCY

Not unless you should find fault without a cause, madam.

MELINDA

Cause or no cause, I must not lose the pleasure of chiding   190
when I please; women must discharge their vapours some-
where, and before we get husbands, our servants must
expect to bear with 'em.

LUCY

Then, madam, you had better raise me to a degree above a
servant: you know my family, and that five hundred pound   195
would set me upon the foot of a gentlewoman, and make me
worthy the confidence of any lady in the land. Besides,
madam, 'twill extremely encourage me in the great design I
now have in hand.

MELINDA

I don't find that your design can be of any great advantage   200
to you; 'twill please me indeed in the humour I have of being
revenged on the fool for his vanity of making love to me, so
I don't much care if I do promise you five hundred pound
upon my day of marriage.

LUCY

That is the way, madam, to make me diligent in the vocation   205
of a confidante, which I think is generally to bring people
together.

MELINDA

Oh, Lucy, I can hold my secret no longer – you must know
that hearing of the famous fortune-teller in town, I went
disguised to satisfy a curiosity which has cost me dear; that   210
fellow is certainly the devil, or one of his bosom favourites,
he has told me the most surprising things of my past life –

LUCY

Things past, madam, can hardly be reckoned surprising,

because we know them already; did he tell you anything
surprising that was to come?   215

LUCY

MELINDA

One thing very surprising, he said I should die a maid.

LUCY

Die a maid! Come into the world for nothing! – Dear
madam, if you should believe him, it might come to pass;
for the bare thought on't might kill one in four and twenty
hours. – And did you ask him any questions about me?   220

MELINDA

You! Why, I passed for you.

LUCY

So 'tis I that am to die a maid – but the devil was a liar from
the beginning, he can't make me die a maid – I have put it
out of his power already.

MELINDA

I do but jest, I would have passed for you, and called myself   225
Lucy, but he presently told me my name, my quality, my
fortune, and gave me the whole history of my life; he told me
of a lover I had in this country, and described Worthy
exactly, but in nothing so well as in his present indifference
– I fled to him for refuge here today – he never so much as   230
encouraged me in my fright, but coldly told me that he was
sorry for the accident, because it might give the town cause
to censure my conduct; excused his not waiting on me home,
made a careless bow, and walked off. 'Sdeath, I could have
stabbed him, or myself, 'twas the same thing. – Yonder he   235
comes – I will so slave him.

LUCY

Don't exasperate him, consider what the fortune-teller told
you; men are scarce, and as times go, it is not impossible for
a woman to die a maid.

Enter WORTHY

MELINDA

No matter.   240

WORTHY

I find she's warmed, I must strike while the iron is hot. –
You have a great deal of courage, madam, to venture into the
walks where you were so late frighted.

MELINDA

And you have a quantity of impudence to appear before me,
that you have so lately affronted.   245

WORTHY

I had no design to affront you, nor appear before you either,
madam; I left you here because I had business in another
place, and came hither thinking to meet another person.

MELINDA

Since you find yourself disappointed, I hope you'll withdraw
to another part of the walk.　　　250

WORTHY

The walk is broad enough for us both. (*They walk by one
another, he with his hat cocked, she fretting and tearing her fan*)
Will you please to take snuff, madam?
*He offers her his box, she strikes it out of his hand; while he is
gathering it up,*

Enter BRAZEN

BRAZEN

What, here before me, my dear!
　　　　　　　Takes MELINDA *round the waist*

MELINDA

What means this insolence?　　　*She cuffs him*

LUCY

(*To* BRAZEN) Are you mad? Don't you see Mr Worthy?　255

BRAZEN

No, no, I'm struck blind – Worthy! – Adso, well turned,
my mistress has wit at her fingers' ends – madam, I ask your
pardon, 'tis our way abroad – Mr Worthy, you're the happy
man.

WORTHY

I don't envy your happiness very much, if the lady can afford　260
no other sort of favours but what she has bestowed upon
you.

MELINDA

I'm sorry the favour miscarried, for it was designed for you,
Mr Worthy; and be assured, 'tis the last and only favour you
must expect at my hands. – Captain, I ask your pardon.　265
　　　　　　　　　　　Exit with LUCY

BRAZEN

I grant it. – You see, Mr Worthy, 'twas only a random shot,
it might ha' taken off your head as well as mine; courage, my
dear, 'tis the fortune of war; but the enemy has thought fit
to withdraw, I think.

WORTHY

Withdraw! Oons, sir, what d'ye mean by withdraw?　270

BRAZEN
    I'll show you.   *Exit*
WORTHY
    She's lost, irrecoverably lost, and Plume's advice has ruined
    me; 'sdeath, why should I that knew her haughty spirit be
    ruled by a man that's a stranger to her pride.

                        Enter PLUME

PLUME
    Ha, ha, ha, a battle royal; don't frown so, man, she's your   275
    own, I tell'ee; I saw the fury of her love in the extremity of
    her passion, the wildness of her anger is a certain sign that
    she loves you to madness. That rogue, Kite, began the
    battle with abundance of conduct, and will bring you off
    victorious, my life on't; he plays his part admirably; she's to   280
    be with him again presently.
WORTHY
    But what could be the meaning of Brazen's familiarity with
    her?
PLUME
    You are no logician if you pretend to draw consequences
    from the actions of fools; there's no arguing by the rule of   285
    reason upon a science without principles, and such is their
    conduct; whim, unaccountable whim, hurries 'em on, like a
    man drunk with brandy before ten o'clock in the morning –
    but we lose our sport; Kite has opened above an hour ago,
    let's away.   *Exeunt*   290

                   [Act IV], Scene ii

                        A Chamber
KITE, *disguised in a strange habit, sitting at a table, [whereon are*
              books and globes; SERVANT in attendance]
KITE (*Rising*)
    By the position of the heavens, gained from my observation
    upon these celestial globes, I find that Luna was a tide-waiter,
    Sol a surveyor, Mercury a thief, Venus a whore, Saturn an
    alderman, Jupiter a rake, and Mars a sergeant of grenadiers;
    and this is the system of Kite the conjurer.   5

                  Enter PLUME *and* WORTHY

PLUME
    Well, what success?

KITE
  I have sent away a shoemaker and a tailor already, one's to be
  a captain of marines and the other a major of dragoons, I am
  to manage them at night. Have you seen the lady, Mr
  Worthy?   10
WORTHY
  Aye, but it won't do – have you showed her her name that I
  tore off from the bottom of the letter?
KITE
  No, sir, I reserve that for the last stroke.
PLUME
  What letter?
WORTHY
  One that I would not let you see, for fear you should break   15
  windows in good earnest.   *Knocking at the door*
KITE
  Officers to your post.   *Exeunt* WORTHY *and* PLUME
  Tycho, mind the door.

            SERVANT *opens the door*, *enter* [THOMAS,] *a* SMITH

SMITH
  Well, master, are you the cunning man?
KITE
  I am the learned Copernicus.   20
SMITH
  Well, Master Coppernose, I'm but a poor man and I can't
  afford above a shilling for my fortune.
KITE
  Perhaps that is more than 'tis worth.
SMITH
  Look'ee, doctor, let me have something that's good for my
  shilling, or I'll have my money again.   25
KITE
  If there be faith in the stars, you shall have your shilling forty
  fold. Your hand, countryman – you are by trade a smith.
SMITH
  How the devil should you know that?
KITE
  Because the devil and you are brother tradesmen – you were
  born under Forceps.   30
SMITH
  Forceps, what's that?
KITE
  One of the signs; there's Leo, Sagittarius, Forceps, Furnes,

Dixmude, Namur, Brussels, Charleroi, and so forth – twelve
of 'em. Let me see – did you ever make any bombs or
cannon-bullets?   35

KITE

Not I.

SMITH

You either have, or will – the stars have decreed that you
shall be – I must have more money, sir, your fortune's great –

SMITH

Faith, doctor, I have no more.

KITE

Oh, sir, I'll trust you, and take it out of your arrears.   40

SMITH

Arrears! What arrears?

KITE

The five hundred pound that's owing to you from the
government.

SMITH

Owing me!

KITE

Owing you, sir – let me see your t'other hand – I beg your   45
pardon, it will be owing to you; and the rogue of an agent
will demand fifty per cent for a fortnight's advance.

SMITH

I'm in the clouds, doctor, all this while.

KITE

Sir, I am above 'em, among the stars – in two years, three
months, and two hours, you will be made Captain of the   50
Forges to the Grand Train of Artillery, and will have ten
shillings a day and two servants; 'tis the decree of the stars,
and of the fixed stars, that are as immovable as your anvil.
Strike, sir, while the iron is hot – fly, sir, begone –

SMITH

What! What would you have me do, doctor? I wish the stars   55
would put me in a way for this fine place.

KITE

The stars do – let me see – aye, about an hour hence walk
carelessly into the market-place and you'll see a tall, slender
gentleman cheapening a pen'worth of apples, with a cane
hanging upon his button – this gentleman will ask you what's   60
o'clock – he's your man, and the maker of your fortune;
follow him, follow him. And now go home and take leave of
your wife and children; an hour hence exactly is your time.

SMITH
A tall, slender gentleman, you say! With a cane. Pray, what
sort of a head has the cane?   65
KITE
An amber head with a black ribband.
SMITH
But pray, of what employment is the gentleman?
KITE
Let me see – he's either a collector of the excise, or a pleni-
potentiary, or a captain of grenadiers – I can't tell exactly
which. But he'll call you honest – your name is –   70
SMITH
Thomas.
KITE
He'll call you honest Tom.
SMITH
But how the devil should he know my name?
KITE
Oh, there are several sorts of Toms – Tom a'Lincoln, Tom-
tit, Tom Telltroth, Tom o'Bedlam, Tom Fool. – (*Knocking*   75
at the door) Begone – an hour hence precisely.
SMITH
You say he'll ask me what's o'clock?
KITE
Most certainly, and you'll answer you don't know, and be
sure you look at St Mary's dial, for the sun won't shine, and
if it should, you won't be able to tell the figures.   80
SMITH
I will, I will.   *Exit*
PLUME ([*Appearing*] *behind*)
Well done, conjurer, go on and prosper.
KITE
As you were.

Enter [PLUCK] *a* BUTCHER

KITE (*Aside*)
What, my old friend Pluck the butcher – I offered the surly
bulldog five guineas this morning and he refused it.   85
BUTCHER
So, Master Conjurer, here's half a crown – and now you
must understand –
KITE
Hold, friend, I know your business beforehand.

BUTCHER

You're devilish cunning then; for I don't well know it myself.

KITE

I know more than you, friend – you have a foolish saying,   90
that such a one knows no more than the man in the moon;
I tell you the man in the moon knows more than all the men
under the sun; don't the moon see all the world?

BUTCHER

All the world see the moon, I must confess.

KITE

Then she must see all the world, that's certain. Give me   95
your hand – you're by trade either a butcher or a surgeon.

BUTCHER

True, I am a butcher.

KITE

And a surgeon you will be, the employments differ only in
the name – he that can cut up an ox, may dissect a man, and
the same dexterity that cracks a marrow-bone will cut off a   100
leg or an arm.

BUTCHER

What d'ye mean, doctor, what d'ye mean?

KITE

Patience, patience, Mr Surgeon-General, the stars are great
bodies and move slowly.

BUTCHER

But what d'ye mean by Surgeon-General, doctor?   105

KITE

Nay, sir, if your worship won't have patience, I must beg the
favour of your worship's absence.

BUTCHER

My worship, my worship! But why my worship?

KITE

Nay, then I have done.   *Sits*

BUTCHER

Pray, doctor.   110

KITE

Fire and fury, sir! (*Rises in a passion*) Do you think the stars
will be hurried? Do the stars owe you any money, sir, that
you dare to dun their lordships at this rate? Sir, I am porter
to the stars, and I am ordered to let no dun come near their
doors.   115

BUTCHER

Dear doctor, I never had any dealings with the stars, they
don't owe me a penny – but since you are their porter, please

to accept of this half-crown to drink their healths, and don't
be angry.

KITE

Let me see your hand then once more – here has been gold –   120
five guineas, my friend, in this very hand this morning.

BUTCHER

Nay, then he is the devil – pray, doctor, were you born of a
woman, or did you come into the world of your own head?

KITE

That's a secret – this gold was offered you by a proper, handsome man, called Hawk, or Buzzard, or –   125

BUTCHER

Kite, you mean.

KITE

Aye, aye, Kite.

BUTCHER

As errant a rogue as ever carried a halberd – the impudent
rascal would have decoyed me for a soldier.

KITE

A soldier! A man of your substance for a soldier! Your   130
mother has a hundred pound in hard money lying at this
minute in the hands of a mercer, not forty yards from this
place.

BUTCHER

Oons, and so she has, but very few know so much.

KITE

I know it, and that rogue, what's his name, Kite, knew it, and 135
offered you five guineas to list because he knew your poor
mother would give the hundred for your discharge.

BUTCHER

There's a dog now – flesh, doctor, I'll give you t'other half-
crown, and tell me that this same Kite will be hanged.

KITE

He's in as much danger as any man in the county of Salop.   140

BUTCHER

There's your fee – but you have forgot the Surgeon-General
all this while.

KITE

You put the stars in a passion.   *Looks on his books*
But now they're pacified again – let me see – did you never
cut off a man's leg?   145

BUTCHER

No.

KITE

Recollect, pray.

BUTCHER

I say no.

KITE

That's strange, wonderful strange; but nothing is strange to me, such wonderful changes have I seen – the second or 150 third, aye, the third campaign that you make in Flanders, the leg of a great officer will be shattered by a great shot; you will be there accidentally, and with your cleaver chop off the limb at a blow; in short, the operation will be performed with so much dexterity, that with general applause you will be made 155 Surgeon-General of the whole army.

BUTCHER

Nay, for the matter of cutting off a limb, I'll do't, I'll do't with any surgeon in Europe, but I have no thoughts of making a campaign.

KITE

You have no thoughts! What matter for your thoughts? The 160 stars have decreed it, and you must go.

BUTCHER

The stars decree it! Oons, sir, the justices can't press me.

KITE

Nay, friend, 'tis none of my business, I ha' done. Only mind this, you'll know more an hour and a half hence – that's all – farewell. *Going* 165

BUTCHER

Hold, hold, doctor, Surgeon-General! What is the place worth, pray?

KITE

Five hundred pound a year, beside guineas for claps.

BUTCHER

Five hundred pound a year! – An hour and half hence you say? 170

KITE

Prithee, friend, be quiet, don't be so troublesome, here's such a work to make a booby butcher accept five hundred pound a year. – But if you must hear it – I tell you in short, you'll be standing in your stall an hour and half hence, and a gentleman will come by with a snuff-box in his hand, and 175 the tip of his handkerchief hanging out of his right pocket; he'll ask you the price of a loin of veal, and at the same time stroke your great dog upon the head and call him Chopper.

BUTCHER
Mercy upon us! Chopper is the dog's name.

KITE
Look'ee there – what I say is true, things that are to come   180
must come to pass. Get you home, sell off your stock, don't
mind the whining and the snivelling of your mother and
your sister, women always hinder preferment; make what
money you can and follow that gentleman, his name begins
with a P – mind that. There will be the barber's daughter,   185
too, that you promised marriage to, she will be pulling and
hauling you to pieces.

BUTCHER
What! Know Sally too? He's the devil, and he needs must
go that the devil drives. – (*Going*) The tip of his handkerchief
out of his left pocket?   190

KITE
No, no, his right pocket; if it be the left, 'tis none of the man.

BUTCHER
Well, well, I'll mind him.   *Exit*

PLUME (*Behind with his pocket-book*)
The right pocket, you say?

KITE
I hear the rustling of silks. (*Knocking*) Fly, sir, 'tis Madam
Melinda.   195

Enter MELINDA *and* LUCY

KITE [*To* SERVANT]
Tycho, chairs for the ladies.

MELINDA
Don't trouble yourself, we shan't stay, doctor.

KITE
Your ladyship is to stay much longer than you imagine.

MELINDA
For what?

KITE
For a husband. – (*To* LUCY) For your part, madam, you   200
won't stay for a husband.

LUCY
Pray, doctor, do you converse with the stars, or with the
devil?

KITE
With both; when I have the destinies of men in search, I
consult the stars; when the affairs of women come under my   205

hand, I advise with my t'other friend.

MELINDA

And have you raised the devil upon my account?

KITE

Yes, madam, and he's now under the table.

LUCY

Oh, heavens protect us! Dear madam, let us be gone.

KITE

If you be afraid of him, why do you come to consult him?   210

MELINDA

Don't fear, fool. Do you think, sir, that because I'm a woman
I'm to be fooled out of my reason, or frighted out of my
senses? – Come, show me this devil.

KITE

He's a little busy at present, but when he has done he shall
wait on you.   215

MELINDA

What is he doing?

KITE

Writing your name in his pocket-book.

MELINDA

Ha, ha, ha, my name! Pray, what have you or he to do with
my name?

KITE

Look'ee, fair lady – the devil is a very modest person, he seeks   220
nobody unless they seek him first; he's chained up like a
mastiff, and can't stir unless he be let loose. – You come to
me to have your fortune told – do you think, madam, that I
can answer you of my own head? No, madam, the affairs of
women are so irregular, that nothing less than the devil can   225
give any account of 'em. Now to convince you of your
incredulity, I'll show you a trial of my skill. – Here, you
Cacodemo del Plumo, exert your power, – draw me this lady's
name, the word Melinda, in the proper letters and character
of her own handwriting. – Do it at three motions – one –   230
two – three – 'tis done – now, madam, will you please to send
your maid to fetch it.

LUCY

I fetch it! The devil fetch me if I do.

MELINDA

My name in my own handwriting! That would be convincing
indeed.   235

KITE

Seeing's believing.   *Goes to the table, lifts up the carpet*
Here Tre, Tre, poor Tre, give me the bone, sirrah. – There's
your name upon that square piece of paper – behold –

MELINDA

'Tis wonderful! My very letters to a tittle.

LUCY

'Tis like your hand, madam, but not so like your hand   240
neither, and now I look nearer, 'tis not like your hand at all.

KITE

Here's a chambermaid now will out-lie the devil.

LUCY

Look'ee, madam, they shan't impose upon us; people can't
remember their hands no more than they can their faces. –
Come, madam, let us be certain, write your name upon this   245
paper, then we'll compare the two names.

                              Takes out paper and folds it

KITE

Anything for your satisfaction, madam – here's pen and ink.

                    MELINDA *writes*, LUCY *holds the paper*

LUCY

Let me see it, madam, 'tis the same, the very same. – (*Aside*)
But I'll secure one copy for my own affairs.

MELINDA

This is demonstration.   250

KITE

'Tis so, madam, the word 'demonstration' comes from
Daemon the father of lies.

MELINDA

Well, doctor, I'm convinced; and now pray what account
can you give me of my future fortune?

KITE

Before the sun has made one course round this earthly globe,   255
your fortune will be fixed for happiness or misery.

MELINDA

What! So near the crisis of my fate!

KITE

Let me see – about the hour of ten tomorrow morning you
will be saluted by a gentleman who will come to take his leave
of you, being designed for travel. His intention of going   260
abroad is sudden, and the occasion a woman. Your fortune
and his are like the bullet and the barrel, one runs plump
into the t'other. – In short, if the gentleman travels he will
die abroad, and if he does you will die before he comes home.

MELINDA
What sort of man is he?   265
KITE
Madam, he's a fine gentleman, and a lover – that is, a man of
very good sense, and a very great fool.
MELINDA
How is that possible, doctor?
KITE
Because, madam – because it is so: a woman's reason is the
best for a man's being a fool.   270
MELINDA
Ten o'clock, you say?
KITE
Ten, about the hour of tea-drinking throughout the kingdom.
MELINDA
Here, doctor. (*Gives money*) Lucy, have you any questions
to ask?
LUCY
Oh, madam! a thousand.   275
KITE
I must beg your patience till another time, for I expect more
company this minute; besides, I must discharge the gentle-
man under the table.
LUCY
Oh, pray, sir, discharge us first.
KITE
Tycho, wait on the ladies downstairs.   280
                                        Exit MELINDA *and* LUCY

                    Enter PLUME *and* WORTHY

KITE
Mr Worthy, you were pleased to wish me joy today, I hope
to be able to return the compliment tomorrow.
WORTHY
I'll make it the best compliment to you that ever I made in
my life, if you do; but I must be a traveller, you say?
KITE
No farther than the chops of the Channel, I presume, sir.   285
PLUME
That we have concerted already. (*Knocking hard*) Hey day!
You don't profess midwifery, doctor?
KITE
Away to your ambuscade.   *Exeunt* PLUME *and* WORTHY

Enter BRAZEN

BRAZEN

Your servant, servant, my dear.

KITE

Stand off, I have my familiar already.   290

BRAZEN

Are you bewitched, my dear?

KITE

Yes, my dear, but mine is a peaceable spirit, and hates
gunpowder – thus I fortify myself; (*draws a circle round
him*) and now, Captain, have a care how you force my lines.

BRAZEN

Lines! What dost talk of lines? You have something like a   295
fishing-rod there, indeed; but I come to be acquainted
with you, man – what's your name, my dear?

KITE

Conundrum.

BRAZEN

Conundrum! Rat me, I know a famous doctor in London of
your name – where were you born?   300

KITE

I was born in Algebra.

BRAZEN

Algebra! – 'Tis no country in Christendom I'm sure,
unless it be some pitiful place in the Highlands of Scotland.

KITE

Right! I told you I was bewitched.

BRAZEN

So am I, my dear, I'm going to be married – I've had two   305
letters from a lady of fortune that loves me to madness, fits,
colic, spleen, and vapours – shall I marry her in four and
twenty hours, aye or no?

KITE

I must have the year and day o'th' month when these
letters were dated.   310

BRAZEN

Why, you old bitch, did you ever hear of love-letters dated
with the year and day o'th' month? Do you think *billets doux*
are like bank bills?

KITE

They are not so good – but if they bear no date, I must
examine the contents.   315

BRAZEN

Contents, that you shall, old boy, [*pulls out two letters*] here
they be both.

KITE

Only the last you received, if you please. (*Takes the letter*)
Now, sir, if you please to let me consult my books for a
minute, I'll send this letter enclosed to you with the deter-   320
mination of the stars upon it to your lodgings.

BRAZEN

With all my heart – I must give him – (*puts his hand in his
pocket*) Algebra! I fancy, doctor, 'tis hard to calculate the
place of your nativity – here. – (*Gives him money*) And if I
succeed, I'll build a watchtower upon the top of the highest   325
mountain in Wales for the study of astrology, and the benefit of Conundrums.   *Exit*

Enter PLUME *and* WORTHY

WORTHY

Oh! Doctor, that letter's worth a million, let me see it –
and now I have it, I'm afraid to open it.

PLUME

Pho, let me see it! (*Opening the letter*) If she be a jilt – damn   330
her, she is one – there's her name at the bottom on't.

WORTHY

How! – Then I'll travel in good earnest – by all my hopes,
'tis Lucy's hand.

PLUME

Lucy's!

WORTHY

Certainly, 'tis no more like Melinda's character than black   335
is to white.

PLUME

Then 'tis certainly Lucy's contrivance to draw in Brazen
for a husband – but are you sure 'tis not Melinda's hand?

WORTHY

You shall see; where's the bit of paper I gave you just now
that the devil writ 'Melinda' upon?   340

KITE

Here, sir.

PLUME

'Tis plain, they're not the same; and is this the malicious
name that was subscribed to the letter which made Mr
Balance send his daughter into the country?

WORTHY
The very same, the other fragments I showed you just now.   345
PLUME
But 'twas barbarous to conceal this so long, and to con-
tinue me so many hours in the pernicious heresy of believing
that angelic creature could change – poor Silvia!
WORTHY
Rich Silvia, you mean, and poor captain – ha, ha, ha; come,
come, friend, Melinda is true and shall be mine; Silvia is   350
constant and may be yours.
PLUME
No, she's above my hopes – but for her sake I'll recant my
opinion of her sex.
   By some the sex is blamed without design,
   Light, harmless censure, such as yours and mine,   355
   Sallies of wit, and vapours of our wine.
   Others the justice of the sex condemn,
   And wanting merit to create esteem,
   Would hide their own defects by censuring them.
   But they, secure in their all-conqu'ring charms,   360
   Laugh at the vain efforts of false alarms;
   He magnifies their conquests who complains,
   For none would struggle were they not in chains.
Exeunt

Act V, Scene i

An Antechamber [adjoining SILVIA's *bedroom], with a
periwig, hat, and sword upon the table
Enter* SILVIA *in her nightcap*

SILVIA
I have rested but indifferently, and I believe my bedfellow
was as little pleased; poor Rose! Here she comes –

Enter ROSE

Good morrow, my dear, how d'ye this morning?
ROSE
Just as I was last night, neither better nor worse for you.
SILVIA
What's the matter? Did you not like your bedfellow?   5
ROSE
I don't know whether I had a bedfellow or not.

SILVIA
  Did not I lie with you?
ROSE
  No – I wonder you could have the conscience to ruin a poor
  girl for nothing.
SILVIA
  I have saved thee from ruin, child; don't be melancholy, I   10
  can give you as many fine things as the captain can.
ROSE
  But you can't, I'm sure.   *Knocking at the door*
SILVIA
  Odso! My accoutrements – (*Puts on her periwig, hat, and
  sword*) Who's at the door?
[CONSTABLE (*without*)]
  Open the door, or we'll break it down.   15
SILVIA
  Patience a little –   *Opens the door*

            Enter [MR BRIDEWELL, *a*] CONSTABLE *and* WATCH

CONSTABLE
  We have 'em, we have 'em, the duck and the mallard both
  in the decoy.
SILVIA
  What means this riot? Stand off! (*Draws*) The man dies
  that comes within reach of my point.   20
CONSTABLE
  That is not the point, master, put up your sword or I shall
  knock you down; and so I command the Queen's peace.
SILVIA
  You are some blockhead of a constable.
CONSTABLE
  I am so, and have a warrant to apprehend the bodies of you
  and your whore there.   25
ROSE
  Whore! Never was poor woman so abused.

            Enter BULLOCK *unbuttoned*

BULLOCK
  What's matter now? – Oh! Mr Bridewell, what brings you
  abroad so early?
CONSTABLE
  This, sir – (*Lays hold of* BULLOCK) You're the Queen's
  prisoner.   . 30

BULLOCK

Wauns, you lie, sir, I'm the Queen's soldier.

CONSTABLE

No matter for that, you shall go before Justice Balance.

SILVIA

Balance! 'Tis what I wanted. – Here, Mr Constable, I resign my sword.

ROSE

Can't you carry us before the captain, Mr Bridewell?   35

CONSTABLE

Captain! Han't you got your bellyful of captains yet? Come, come, make way there.   *Exeunt*

[Act V], Scene ii

JUSTICE BALANCE's *house*
Enter BALANCE *and* SCALE

SCALE

I say 'tis not to be borne, Mr Balance.

BALANCE

Look'ee, Mr Scale, for my own part I shall be very tender in what regards the officers of the army; they expose their lives to so many dangers for us abroad that we may give them some grains of allowance at home.   5

SCALE

Allowance! This poor girl's father is my tenant, and if I mistake not, her mother nursed a child for you; shall they debauch our daughters to our faces?

BALANCE

Consider, Mr Scale, that were it not for the bravery of these officers we should have French dragoons among us, that   10 would leave us neither liberty, property, wife, nor daughter. – Come, Mr Scale, the gentlemen are vigorous and warm, and may they continue so; the same heat that stirs them up to love, spurs them on to battle; you never knew a great general in your life that did not love a whore. This I   15 only speak in reference to Captain Plume, for the other spark I know nothing of.

SCALE

Nor can I hear of anybody that does – oh, here they come.
Enter SILVIA, BULLOCK, ROSE, *prisoners*; CONSTABLE *and*
WATCH

CONSTABLE

May it please your worships, we took them in the very act,
re infecta, sir – the gentleman indeed behaved himself like   20
a gentleman, for he drew his sword and swore, and afterwards laid it down and said nothing.

BALANCE

Give the gentleman his sword again – wait you without.

Exeunt CONSTABLE *and* WATCH

(*To* SILVIA) I'm sorry, sir, to know a gentleman upon such
terms, that the occasion of our meeting should prevent the   25
satisfaction of an acquaintance.

SILVIA

Sir, you need make no apology for your warrant, no more
than I shall do for my behaviour – my innocence is upon an
equal foot with your authority.

SCALE

Innocence! Have you not seduced that young maid?   30

SILVIA

No, Mr Goosecap, she seduced me.

BULLOCK

So she did, I'll swear – for she proposed marriage first.

BALANCE

What! Then you're married, child?   (*To* ROSE)

ROSE

Yes, sir, to my sorrow.

BALANCE

Who was witness?   35

BULLOCK

That was I – I danced, threw the stocking, and spoke jokes
by their bedside, I'm sure.

BALANCE

Who was the minister?

BULLOCK

Minister! We are soldiers, and want no ministers – they
were married by the Articles of War.   40

BALANCE

Hold thy prating, fool. Your appearance, sir, promises
some understanding; pray, what does this fellow mean?

SILVIA

He means marriage, I think – but that, you know, is so odd
a thing, that hardly any two people under the sun agree in
the ceremony; some make it a sacrament, others a con-   45
venience, and others make it a jest; but among soldiers
'tis most sacred – our sword, you know, is our honour; that

we lay down, the hero jumps over it first, and the amazon
after – leap rogue, follow whore – the drum beats a ruff,   50
and so to bed; that's all, the ceremony is concise.
BULLOCK
And the prettiest ceremony, so full of pastime and prod-
igality –
BALANCE
What! Are you a soldier?
BULLOCK
Aye, that I am. Will your worship lend me your cane, and
I'll show you how I can exercise.   55
BALANCE
Take it. (*Strikes him over the head*) Pray, sir, what com-
mission may you bear?   (*To* SILVIA)
SILVIA
I'm called Captain, sir, by all the coffeemen, drawers,
whores, and groom-porters in London, for I wear a red
coat, a sword, a hat *bien troussé*, a martial twist in my cravat, 60
a fierce knot in my periwig, a cane upon my button, piquet
in my head, and dice in my pocket.
SCALE
Your name, pray, sir?
SILVIA
Captain Pinch; I cock my hat with a pinch, I take snuff
with a pinch, pay my whores with a pinch; in short, I can   65
do anything at a pinch, but fight and fill my belly.
BALANCE
And pray, sir, what brought you into Shropshire?
SILVIA
A pinch, sir: I knew you country gentlemen want wit, and
you know that we town gentlemen want money, and so –
BALANCE
I understand you, sir. – Here, Constable!   70

Enter CONSTABLE

Take this gentleman into custody till farther orders.
ROSE
Pray your worship, don't be uncivil to him, for he did me no
hurt; he's the most harmless man in the world, for all he
talks so.
SCALE
Come, come, child, I'll take care of you.   75
SILVIA
What, gentlemen, rob me of my freedom and my wife at

once! 'Tis the first time they ever went together.

BALANCE (*Whispers*)

Hark'ee, Constable –

CONSTABLE

It shall be done, sir. – Come along, sir.

Exeunt CONSTABLE, BULLOCK, [ROSE] *and* SILVIA

BALANCE

Come, Mr Scale, we'll manage the spark presently.   80

Exeunt BALANCE *and* SCALE

[Act V], Scene iii
MELINDA'*s Apartment*
Enter MELINDA *and* WORTHY

MELINDA

(*Aside*) So far the prediction is right, 'tis ten exactly. –
And pray sir, how long have you been in this travelling
humour?

WORTHY

'Tis natural, madam, for us to avoid what disturbs our quiet.

MELINDA

Rather the love of change, which is more natural, may be the   5
occasion of it.

WORTHY

To be sure, madam, there must be charms in variety, else
neither you nor I should be so fond of it.

MELINDA

You mistake, Mr Worthy, I am not so fond of variety as to
travel for't, nor do I think it prudence in you to run your-   10
self into a certain expense and danger, in hopes of pre-
carious pleasures which at best never answer expectation,
as 'tis evident from the example of most travellers, that
long more to return to their own country than they did to
go abroad.   15

WORTHY

What pleasures I may receive abroad are indeed uncertain;
but this I am sure of, I shall meet with less cruelty among
the most barbarous nations than I have found at home.

MELINDA

Come, sir, you and I have been jangling a great while; I
fancy if we made up our accounts, we should the sooner   20
come to an agreement.

WORTHY

Sure, madam, you won't dispute your being in my debt –

my fears, sighs, vows, promises, assiduities, anxieties,
jealousies, have run on for a whole year, without any pay-
ment.   25

MELINDA
A year! Oh Mr Worthy, what you owe to me is not to be
paid under a seven years' servitude. How did you use me the
year before, when taking the advantage of my innocence and
necessity, you would have made me your mistress, that is,
your slave? Remember the wicked insinuations, artful baits,   30
deceitful arguments, cunning pretences; then your impudent behaviour, loose expressions, familiar letters, rude
visits; remember those, those, Mr Worthy.

WORTHY
(*Aside*) I do remember, and am sorry I made no better use
of 'em. – But you may remember, madam, that –   35

MELINDA
Sir, I'll remember nothing – 'tis your interest that I should
forget; you have been barbarous to me, I have been cruel to
you; put that and that together, and let one balance the
other. Now if you will begin upon a new score, lay aside
your adventuring airs, and behave yourself handsomely till   40
Lent be over, here's my hand, I'll use you as a gentleman
should be.

WORTHY
And if I don't use you as a gentlewoman should be, may
this be my poison.   *Kissing her hand*

                         Enter SERVANT

SERVANT
Madam, the coach is at the door.   45

MELINDA
I'm going to Mr Balance's country-house to see my cousin
Silvia; I have done her an injury, and can't be easy till I have
asked her pardon.

WORTHY
I dare not hope for the honour of waiting on you.

MELINDA
My coach is full, but if you will be so gallant as to mount   50
your own horses and follow us, we shall be glad to be
overtaken; and if you bring Captain Plume with you, we
shan't have the worse reception.

WORTHY
I'll endeavour it.   *Exit* WORTHY *leading* MELINDA

[Act V], Scene iv
The Market-place
Enter PLUME *and* KITE

PLUME
A baker, a tailor, a smith, and a butcher – I believe the first
colony planted at Virginia had not more trades in their
company than I have in mine.

KITE
The butcher, sir, will have his hands full; for we have two
sheep stealers among us – I hear of a fellow, too, com-   5
mitted just now for stealing of horses.

PLUME
We'll dispose of him among the dragoons. Have we ne'er a
poulterer among us?

KITE
Yes, sir, the king of the gypsies is a very good one, he has an
excellent hand at a goose or a turkey. Here's Captain Brazen,   10
sir – I must go look after the men.   *Exit*

Enter BRAZEN *reading a letter*

BRAZEN
Um, um, um, the canonical hour – um, um, very well. – My
dear Plume! Give me a buss.

PLUME
Half a score if you will, my dear. [*They kiss*] What hast got
in thy hand, child?   15

BRAZEN
'Tis a project for laying out a thousand pound.

PLUME
Were it not requisite to project first how to get it in?

BRAZEN
You can't imagine, my dear, that I want a thousand pound;
I have spent twenty times as much in the service – now, my
dear, pray advise me, my head runs much upon architec-   20
ture; shall I build a privateer or a playhouse?

PLUME
An odd question – a privateer or a playhouse! 'Twill require
some consideration. – Faith, I'm for a privateer.

BRAZEN
I'm not of your opinion, my dear – for in the first place a
privateer may be ill-built.   25

PLUME
And so may a playhouse.
BRAZEN
But a privateer may be ill-manned.
PLUME
And so may a playhouse.
BRAZEN
But a privateer may run upon the shallows.
PLUME
Not so often as a playhouse.   30
BRAZEN
But, you know, a privateer may spring a leak.
PLUME
And I know that a playhouse may spring a great many.
BRAZEN
But suppose the privateer come home with a rich booty, we
should never agree about our shares.
PLUME
'Tis just so in a playhouse – so by my advice, you shall fix   35
upon the privateer.
BRAZEN
Agreed – but if this twenty thousand should not be in
specie –
PLUME
What twenty thousand?
BRAZEN
Hark'ee –   *Whispers*   40
PLUME
Married!
BRAZEN
Presently, we're to meet about half a mile out of town at the
waterside – and so forth – (*Reads*) 'For fear I should be
known by any of Worthy's friends, you must give me leave
to wear my mask till after the ceremony, which will make me 45
ever yours'. – Look'ee there, my dear dog –
                Shows the bottom of the letter to PLUME
PLUME
Melinda! And by this light, her own hand! – Once more, if
you please, my dear; her hand exactly! – Just now you say?
BRAZEN
This minute I must be gone.
PLUME
Have a little patience, and I'll go with you.   50

BRAZEN

No, no, I see a gentleman coming this way that may be inquisitive; 'tis Worthy, do you know him?

PLUME

By sight only.

BRAZEN

Have a care, the very eyes discover secrets –   *Exit*

Enter WORTHY

WORTHY

To boot and saddle, Captain, you must mount.   55

PLUME

Whip and spur, Worthy, or you won't mount.

WORTHY

But I shall: Melinda and I are agreed; she's gone to visit Silvia, we are to mount and follow, and could we carry a parson with us, who knows what might be done for us both?

PLUME

Don't trouble your head, Melinda has secured a parson   60 already.

WORTHY

Already! Do you know more than I?

PLUME

Yes, I saw it under her hand – Brazen and she are to meet half a mile hence at the waterside, there to take boat, I suppose to be ferried over to the Elysian fields, if there be any   65 such thing in matrimony.

WORTHY

I parted with Melinda just now; she assured me she hated Brazen, and that she resolved to discard Lucy for daring to write letters to him in her name.

PLUME

Nay, nay, there's nothing of Lucy in this – I tell ye I saw   70 Melinda's hand as surely as this is mine.

WORTHY

But I tell you, she's gone this minute to Justice Balance's country-house.

PLUME

But I tell you, she's gone this minute to the waterside.

Enter a SERVANT

SERVANT (*to* WORTHY)

Madam Melinda has sent word that you need not trouble   75 yourself to follow her, because her journey to Justice

Balance's is put off, and she's gone to take the air another
way.

WORTHY

How! Her journey put off?

PLUME

That is, her journey was a put-off to you.   80

WORTHY

'Tis plain, plain – but how, where, when is she to meet
Brazen?

PLUME

Just now, I tell you, half a mile hence at the waterside.

WORTHY

Up, or down the water?

PLUME

That I don't know.   85

WORTHY

I'm glad my horses are ready. – Jack, get 'em out.
                                        [*Exit* SERVANT]

PLUME

Shall I go with you?

WORTHY

Not an inch; I shall return presently.

PLUME

You'll find me at the hall; the justices are sitting by this
time, and I must attend them.   [*Exeunt severally*]   90

[Act V], Scene v

A Court of Justice
BALANCE, SCALE *and* SCRUPLE *upon the bench;*
CONSTABLE, KITE, *Mob [in attendance]*
KITE *and* CONSTABLE *advance forward*

KITE

Pray, who are those honourable gentlemen upon the bench?

CONSTABLE

He in the middle is Justice Balance, he on the right is
Justice Scale, and he on the left is Justice Scruple, and I
am Mr Constable, four very honest gentlemen.

KITE

Oh dear sir, I'm your most obedient servant. (*Saluting the*   5
CONSTABLE) I fancy, sir, that your employment and mine are
much the same, for my business is to keep people in order,
and if they disobey, to knock 'em down; and then we're
both staff-officers.

CONSTABLE

Nay, I'm a sergeant myself – of the militia. Come, brother,   10
you shall see me exercise – suppose this a musket now.
(*He puts his staff on his right shoulder*) Now I'm shouldered.

KITE

Aye, you're shouldered pretty well for a constable's staff,
but for a musket you must put it on t'other shoulder, my
dear.   15

CONSTABLE

Adso! That's true. – Come, now give the word o'command.

KITE

Silence.

CONSTABLE

Aye, aye, so we will, – we will be silent.

KITE

Silence, you dog, silence –

Strikes him over the head with his halberd

CONSTABLE

That's the way to silence a man with a witness! – What d'ye   20
mean, friend?

KITE

Only to exercise you, sir.

CONSTABLE

Your exercise differs so from ours, that we shall ne'er agree
about it; if my own captain had given me such a rap, I had
taken the law of him.   25

Enter PLUME

BALANCE

Captain, you're welcome.

PLUME

Gentlemen, I thank'ee.

SCRUPLE

Come, honest Captain, sit by me. (PLUME *ascends, and sits
upon the bench*) Now produce your prisoners – here, that
fellow there – set him up. [CONSTABLE *brings first prisoner to*   30
the dock] Mr Constable, what have you to say against this
man?

CONSTABLE

I have nothing to say against him, an't please ye.

BALANCE

No? What made you bring him hither?

CONSTABLE

I don't know, an't please your worship.   35

SCRUPLE

Did not the contents of your warrant direct you what sort of men to take up?

CONSTABLE

I can't tell, an't please ye, I can't read.

SCRUPLE

A very pretty constable truly! I find we have no business here.   40

KITE

May it please the worshipful bench, I desire to be heard in this case, as being counsel for the Queen.

BALANCE

Come, Sergeant, you shall be heard, since nobody else will speak; we won't come here for nothing.

KITE

This man is but one man, the country may spare him and   45
the army wants him; besides, he's cut out by nature for a grenadier: he's five foot ten inches high, he shall box, wrestle, or dance the Cheshire Round with any man in the county, he gets drunk every sabbath-day, and he beats his wife.   50

WIFE

You lie, sirrah, you lie, an't please your worship, he's the best-natured, pains-taking man in the parish, witness my five poor children.

SCRUPLE

A wife! And five children! You, Constable, you rogue, how durst you impress a man that has a wife and five children?   55

SCALE

Discharge him, discharge him.

BALANCE

Hold, gentlemen. – Hark'ee, friend, how do you maintain your wife and five children?

KITE

They live upon wild fowl and venison, sir; the husband keeps a gun, and kills all the hares and partridges within   60
five mile round.

BALANCE

A gun! Nay, if he be so good at gunning he shall have enough on't – he may be of use against the French, for he shoots flying to be sure.

SCRUPLE

But his wife and children, Mr Balance!   65

WIFE

Aye, aye, that's the reason you would send him away: you know I have a child every year, and you're afraid they should come upon the parish at last.

PLUME

Look'ee there, gentlemen, the honest woman has spoke it at once; the parish had better maintain five children this year   70
than six or seven the next; that fellow upon his high feeding may get you two or three beggars at a birth.

WIFE

Look'ee, Mr Captain, the parish shall get nothing by sending him away, for I won't lose my teeming-time if there be a man left in the parish.   75

BALANCE

Send that woman to the house of correction – and the man –

KITE

I'll take care o'him, if you please.   *Takes him down*

SCALE

Here, you Constable, the next: set up that black-faced fellow, he has a gunpowder look; [CONSTABLE *sets up* SECOND PRISONER] what can you say against this man, Constable?   80

CONSTABLE

Nothing, but that he's a very honest man.

PLUME

Pray, gentlemen, let me have one honest man in my company for the novelty's sake.

BALANCE

What are you, friend?

SECOND PRISONER

A collier, I work in the coal-pits.   85

SCRUPLE

Look'ee, gentlemen, this fellow has a trade, and the Act of Parliament here expresses, that we are to impress no man that has any visible means of a livelihood.

KITE

May it please your worships, this man has no visible means of a livelihood, for he works underground.   90

PLUME

Well said, Kite – Besides, the army wants miners.

BALANCE

Right! And had we an order of government for't, we could raise you in this and the neighbouring county of Stafford five hundred colliers that would run you underground like

moles, and do more service in a siege that all the miners in   95
the army.

SCRUPLE

Well, friend, what have you to say for yourself?

SECOND PRISONER

I'm married.

KITE

Lack-a-day, so am I.

SECOND PRISONER

Here's my wife, poor woman.   100

BALANCE

Are you married, good woman?

WOMAN

I'm married in conscience.

KITE

May it please your worship, she's with child in conscience.

SCALE

Who married you, mistress?

WOMAN

My husband – we agreed that I should call him husband to   105
avoid passing for a whore, and that he should call me wife to
shun going for a soldier.

SCRUPLE

A very pretty couple! Pray, Captain, will you take 'em both?

PLUME

What say you, Mr Kite – will you take care of the woman?

KITE

Yes, sir, she shall go with us to the seaside and there if she   110
has a mind to drown herself we'll take care that nobody
shall hinder her. [*Takes down* SECOND PRISONER]

BALANCE

Here, Constable, bring in my man.   *Exit* CONSTABLE
Now, Captain, I'll fit you with a man such as you ne'er listed
in your life.   115

Enter CONSTABLE *and* SILVIA

Oh my friend Pinch, I'm very glad to see you.

SILVIA

Well, sir, and what then?

SCALE

What then! Is that your respect to the bench?

SILVIA

Sir, I don't care a farthing for you nor your bench neither.

SCRUPLE
>Look'ee, gentlemen, that's enough, he's a very impudent   120
fellow, and fit for a soldier.

SCALE
>A notorious rogue, I say, and very fit for a soldier.

CONSTABLE
>A whoremaster, I say, and therefore fit to go.

BALANCE
>What think you, Captain?

PLUME
>I think he's a very pretty fellow, and therefore fit to serve.   125

SILVIA
>Me for a soldier! Send your own lazy, lubberly sons at home,
fellows that hazard their necks every day in pursuit of a fox,
yet dare not peep abroad to look an enemy in the face.

CONSTABLE
>May it please your worships, I have a woman at the door to
swear a rape against this rogue.   130

SILVIA
>Is it your wife or daughter, booby? I ravished 'em both
yesterday.

BALANCE
>Pray, Captain, read the Articles of War, we'll see him listed
immediately.

PLUME (*Reads*)
>'Articles of War against Mutiny and Desertion . . .'   135

SILVIA
>Hold, sir. – Once more, gentlemen, have a care what you do,
for you shall severely smart for any violence you offer to me;
and you, Mr Balance, I speak to you particularly, you shall
heartily repent it.

PLUME
>Look'ee, young spark, say but one word more and I'll build   140
a horse for you as high as the ceiling, and make you ride the
most tiresome journey that ever you made in your life.

SILVIA
>You have made a fine speech, good Captain Huffcap, but you
had better be quiet, I shall find a way to cool your courage.

PLUME
>Pray, gentlemen, don't mind him, he's distracted.   145

SILVIA
>'Tis false – I'm descended of as good a family as any in your
county, my father is as good a man as any upon your bench,
and I am heir to twelve hundred pound a year.

BALANCE
He's certainly mad – pray, Captain, read the Articles of War.
SILVIA
Hold, once more. – Pray, Mr Balance, to you I speak: sup-   150
pose I were your child, would you use me at this rate?
BALANCE
No, faith, were you mine, I would send you to Bedlam first,
and into the army afterwards.
SILVIA
But consider my father, sir, he's as good, as generous, as
brave, as just a man as ever served his country; I'm his only   155
child, perhaps the loss of me may break his heart.
BALANCE
He's a very great fool if it does. Captain, if you don't list
him this minute I'll leave the court.
PLUME
Kite, do you distribute the levy-money to the men whilst I
read.   160
KITE
Aye, sir, – silence, gentlemen.
                                    PLUME *reads the Articles of War*
BALANCE
Very well; now, Captain, let me beg the favour of you not to
discharge this fellow upon any account whatsoever. –
Bring in the rest.
CONSTABLE
There are no more, an't please your worship.   165
BALANCE
No more! There were five two hours ago.
SILVIA
'Tis true, sir, but this rogue of a constable let the rest escape
for a bribe of eleven shillings a man, because he said that the
Act allows him but ten, so the odd shilling was clear gains.
ALL JUSTICES
How!   170
SILVIA
Gentlemen, he offered to let me get away for two guineas,
but I had not so much about me. – This is truth, and I'm
ready to swear it.
KITE
And I'll swear it, give me the book, 'tis for the good of the
service.   175
SECOND PRISONER
May it please your worship, I gave him half a crown to say

that I was an honest man, – but now since that your worships have made me a rogue, I hope I shall have my money
again.

BALANCE

'Tis my opinion that this constable be put into the captain's   180
hands, and if his friends don't bring four good men for his
ransom by tomorrow night – Captain, you shall carry him to
Flanders.

SCALE, SCRUPLE

Agreed, agreed.

PLUME

Mr Kite, take the constable into custody.   185

KITE

Aye, aye, sir. – (*To the* CONSTABLE) Will you please to have
your office taken from you, or will you handsomely lay
down your staff as your betters have done before you?

                                The CONSTABLE *drops his staff*

BALANCE

Come, gentlemen, there needs no great ceremony in adjourn-
ing this court; – Captain, you shall dine with me.   190

KITE

Come Mr Militia Sergeant, I shall silence you now I
believe, without your taking the law of me.

                                          Exeunt omnes

[Act V], Scene vi

The Fields
Enter BRAZEN *leading in* LUCY *masked*

BRAZEN

The boat is just below here.

            Enter WORTHY *with a case of pistols under his arm*

WORTHY

Here, sir, take your choice.

            Going between 'em, and offering them

BRAZEN

What! Pistols! Are they charged, my dear?

WORTHY

With a brace of bullets each.

BRAZEN

But I'm a foot-officer, my dear, and never use pistols, the   5
sword is my way – and I won't be put out of my road to
please any man.

WORTHY

Nor I neither, so have at you.   *Cocks one pistol*

BRAZEN

Look'ee, my dear, I don't care for pistols; – pray oblige me
and let us have a bout at sharps; damn't there's no parrying   10
these bullets.

WORTHY

Sir, if you han't your belly full of these, the swords shall
come in for second course.

BRAZEN

Why then fire and fury! I have eaten smoke from the mouth
of a cannon, sir, don't think I fear powder, for I live upon't.   15
Let me see. (*Takes one*) And now, sir, how many paces
distant shall we fire?

WORTHY

Fire you when you please, I'll reserve my shot till I be sure
of you.

BRAZEN

Come, where's your cloak?   20

WORTHY

Cloak! What d'ye mean?

BRAZEN

To fight upon, I always fight upon a cloak, 'tis our way
abroad.

LUCY

Come, gentlemen, I'll end the strife.   *Unmasks*

WORTHY

Lucy! Take her.   25

BRAZEN

The devil take me if I do – Huzza! (*Fires his pistol*) D'ye
hear, d'ye hear, you plaguey harridan, how those bullets
whistle, suppose they had been lodged in my gizzard
now? –

LUCY

Pray, sir, pardon me.   30

BRAZEN

I can't tell, child, till I know whether my money be safe.
(*Searching his pockets*) Yes, yes, I do pardon you, – but if I
had you in the Rose Tavern, Covent Garden, with three or
four hearty rakes, and three or four smart napkins, I would
tell you another story, my dear.   *Exit*   35

WORTHY

And was Melinda privy to this?

LUCY

No, sir; she wrote her name upon a piece of paper at the fortune-teller's last night, which I put in my pocket, and so writ above it to the captain.

WORTHY

And how came Melinda's journey put off?   40

LUCY

At the town's end she met Mr Balance's steward, who told her that Mrs Silvia was gone from her father's, and nobody could tell whither.

WORTHY

Silvia gone from her father's! This will be news to Plume. Go home, and tell your lady how near I was being shot for   45
her.   *Exeunt*

[Act V], Scene vii
[BALANCE'*s house*]
Enter BALANCE *with a napkin in his hand, as risen from dinner, and* STEWARD

STEWARD

We did not miss her till the evening, sir, and then searching for her in the chamber that was my young master's, we found her clothes there, but the suit that your son left in the press when he went to London was gone.

BALANCE

The white, trimmed with silver!   5

STEWARD

The same.

BALANCE

You han't told that circumstance to anybody?

STEWARD

To none but your worship.

BALANCE

And be sure you don't. Go into the dining-room, and tell Captain Plume that I beg to speak with him.   10

STEWARD

I shall.   *Exit*

BALANCE

Was ever man so imposed upon? I had her promise indeed that she should never dispose of herself without my consent. – I have consented with a witness, given her away as my act and deed – and this, I warrant, the captain thinks will pass;   15

no, I shall never pardon him the villainy, first of robbing me
of my daughter, and then the mean opinion he must have of
me to think that I could be so wretchedly imposed upon; her
extravagant passion might encourage her in the attempt, but
the contrivance must be his – I'll know the truth presently.   20

Enter PLUME

Pray, Captain, what have you done with your young
gentleman soldier?
PLUME
He's at my quarters, I suppose, with the rest of my men.
BALANCE
Does he keep company with the common soldiers?
PLUME
No, he's generally with me.   25
BALANCE
He lies with you, I presume?
PLUME
No, faith, – I offered him part of my bed, but the young
rogue fell in love with Rose, and has lain with her, I think,
since he came to town.
BALANCE
So that between you both, Rose has been finely managed.   30
PLUME
Upon my honour, sir, she had no harm from me.
BALANCE
All's safe, I find. – Now, Captain, you must know that the
young fellow's impudence in court was well grounded; he
said I should heartily repent his being listed, and so I do
from my soul.   35
PLUME
Aye! For what reason?
BALANCE
Because he is no less than what he said he was, born of as
good a family as any in this county, and is heir to twelve
hundred pound a year.
PLUME
I'm very glad to hear it, for I wanted but a man of that   40
quality to make my company a perfect representative of the
whole commons of England.
BALANCE
Won't you discharge him?
PLUME
Not under a hundred pound sterling.

BALANCE

You shall have it, for his father is my intimate friend.   45

PLUME

Then you shall have him for nothing.

BALANCE

Nay, sir, you shall have your price.

PLUME

Not a penny, sir; I value an obligation to you much above a
hundred pound.

BALANCE

Perhaps, sir, you shan't repent your generosity. – Will you   50
please to write his discharge in my pocket-book? (*Gives his
book*) In the meantime we'll send for the gentleman. Who
waits there?

Enter SERVANT

Go to the captain's lodgings and inquire for Mr Wilful; tell
him his captain wants him here immediately.   55

SERVANT

Sir, the gentleman's below at the door inquiring for the
captain.

PLUME

Bid him come up – here's the discharge, sir.

BALANCE

Sir, I thank you. – (*Aside*) 'Tis plain he had no hand in't.

Enter SILVIA

SILVIA

I think, Captain, you might have used me better, than to   60
leave me yonder among your swearing, drunken crew; and
you, Mr Justice, might have been so civil as to have invited
me to dinner, for I have eaten with as good a man as your
worship.

PLUME

Sir, you must charge our want of respect upon our ignorance   65
of your quality – but now you're at liberty – I have
discharged you.

SILVIA

Discharged me!

BALANCE

Yes, sir, and you must once more go home to your father.

SILVIA

My father! Then I'm discovered! Oh sir, (*kneeling*) I expect   70
no pardon.

BALANCE

Pardon! No, no, child; your crime shall be your punishment;
here, Captain, I deliver her over to the conjugal power for
her chastisement; since she will be a wife, be you a husband,
a very husband: when she tells you of her love, upbraid her　75
with her folly; be modishly ungrateful, because she has been
unfashionably kind; and use her worse than you would
anybody else, because you can't use her so well as she
deserves.

PLUME

And are you Silvia in good earnest?　　　　　　　　　　　80

SILVIA

Earnest! I have gone too far to make it a jest, sir.

PLUME

And do you give her to me in good earnest?

BALANCE

If you please to take her, sir.

PLUME

Why then I have saved my legs and arms, and lost my
liberty; secure from wounds, I'm prepared for the gout;　85
farewell subsistence and welcome taxes. – Sir, my liberty
and hopes of being a general are much dearer to me than
your twelve hundred pound a year – but to your love,
madam, I resign my freedom, and to your beauty my
ambition – greater in obeying at your feet, than commanding　90
at the head of an army.

Enter WORTHY

WORTHY

I'm sorry to hear, Mr Balance, that your daughter is lost.

BALANCE

So am not I, sir, since an honest gentleman has found her.

Enter MELINDA

MELINDA

Pray, Mr Balance, what's become of my cousin Silvia?

BALANCE

Your cousin Silvia is talking yonder with your cousin Plume.　95

MELINDA ⎱
WORTHY ⎰

How!

SILVIA

Do you think it strange, cousin, that a woman should change?
But, I hope, you'll excuse a change that has proceeded from
constancy; I altered my outside because I was the same

within, and only laid by the woman to make sure of my man; 100
that's my history.

MELINDA

Your history is a little romantic, cousin, but since success has
crowned your adventures you will have the world o' your
side, and I shall be willing to go with the tide, provided you
pardon an injury I offered you in the letter to your father. 105

PLUME

That injury, madam, was done to me, and the reparation I
expect shall be made to my friend; make Mr Worthy happy,
and I shall be satisfied.

MELINDA

A good example, sir, will go a great way – when my cousin is
pleased to surrender, 'tis probable I shan't hold out much 110
longer.

Enter BRAZEN

BRAZEN

Gentlemen, I am yours – madam, I am not yours.

MELINDA

I'm glad on't, sir.

BRAZEN

So am I. – You have got a pretty house here, Mr Laconic.

BALANCE

'Tis time to right all mistakes – my name, sir, is Balance. 115

BRAZEN

Balance! Sir, I'm your most obedient. – I know your whole
generation – had not you an uncle that was governor of the
Leeward Islands some years ago?

BALANCE

Did you know him?

BRAZEN

Intimately, sir – he played at billiards to a miracle; you had 120
a brother, too, that was captain of a fireship – poor Dick – he
had the most engaging way with him – of making punch, –
and then his cabin was so neat – but his boy Jack was the most
comical bastard – ha, ha, ha, ha, a pickled dog, I shall never
forget him. 125

PLUME

Well, Captain, are you fixed in your project yet? Are you
still for the privateer?

BRAZEN

No, no, I had enough of a privateer just now, I had like to
have been picked up by a cruiser under false colours, and a
French picaroon for aught I know. 130

PLUME

But have you got your recruits, my dear?

BRAZEN

Not a stick, my dear.

PLUME

Probably I shall furnish you.

Enter ROSE *and* BULLOCK

ROSE

Captain, Captain, I have got loose once more, and have
persuaded my sweetheart Cartwheel to go with us, but you   135
must promise not to part with me again.

SILVIA

I find Mrs Rose has not been pleased with her bedfellow.

ROSE

Bedfellow! I don't know whether I had a bedfellow or not.

SILVIA

Don't be in a passion, child, I was as little pleased with your
company as you could be with mine.   140

BULLOCK

Pray, sir, dunna be offended at my sister, she's something
underbred – but if you please I'll lie with you in her stead.

PLUME

I have promised, madam, to provide for this girl; now will
you be pleased to let her wait upon you, or shall I take care
of her?   145

SILVIA

She shall be my charge, sir, you may find it business enough
to take care of me.

BULLOCK

Aye, and of me, Captain, for wauns! if ever you lift your
hand against me, I'll desert.

PLUME

Captain Brazen shall take care o' that. – My dear, instead of 150
the twenty thousand pound you talked of, you shall have the
twenty brave recruits that I have raised, at the rate they
cost me. – My commission I lay down to be taken up by
some braver fellow, that has more merit and less good
fortune, whilst I endeavour by the example of this worthy   155
gentleman to serve my Queen and country at home.

    With some regret I quit the active field,
    Where glory full reward for life does yield;
    But the recruiting trade, with all its train
    Of lasting plague, fatigue, and endless pain,   160

I gladly quit, with my fair spouse to stay,
And raise recruits the matrimonial way.

Exeunt

EPILOGUE

All ladies and gentlemen that are willing to see the comedy
called *The Recruiting Officer*, let them repair tomorrow night by
six o'clock to the sign of the Theatre Royal in Drury Lane, and
they shall be kindly entertained –

We scorn the vulgar ways to bid you come,   5
Whole Europe now obeys the call of drum.
The soldier, not the poet, here appears,
And beats up for a corps of volunteers;
He finds that music chiefly does delight ye,
And therefore chooses music to invite ye.   10

Beat the *Grenadier March* – Row, row, tow! – Gentlemen,
this piece of music, called *An Overture to a Battle*, was com-
posed by a famous Italian master, and was performed with
wonderful success, at the great operas of Vigo, Schellenberg,
and Blenheim; it came off with the applause of all Europe,   15
excepting France; the French found it a little too rough for
their *delicatesse*.

Some that have acted on those glorious stages,
Are here to witness to succeeding ages
That no music like the *Grenadier's* engages.   20

Ladies, we must own that this music of ours is not altogether
so soft as Bononcini's, yet we dare affirm, that it has laid more
people asleep than all the *Camillas* in the world; and you'll
condescend to own that it keeps one awake better than any
opera that ever was acted.   25
The *Grenadier March* seems to be a composure excellently
adapted to the genius of the English; for no music was ever
followed so far by us, nor with so much alacrity; and with all
deference to the present subscription, we must say that the
Grenadier March has been subscribed for by the whole Grand   30
Alliance; and we presume to inform the ladies, that it always
has the pre-eminence abroad, and is constantly heard by the
tallest, handsomest men in the whole army. In short, to gratify
the present taste, our author is now adapting some words to
the *Grenadier March*, which he intends to have performed   35
tomorrow, if the lady who is to sing it should not happen to be
sick.

This he concludes to be the surest way
To draw you hither, for you'll all obey
Soft music's call, though you should damn his play.   40